ANXIETY & DEPRESSION

CBT with a 2 in 1 book guide to Manage Negative Thoughts and Build Emotional Control

Daniel Mercer

ISBN: 9781807652555

Published by TPSA Publishing

Table of Contents

BOOK 1 - Cognitive Behavioral Therapy for Anxiety

7 Techniques of CBT for Overcome Anger, Negative Thoughts, Insomnia and Decluttering your Brain. Made Simple Guide to Improve your Freedom from Social Anxiety

Daniel Mercer

Introduction

A human being is structured in a way that he or she is not to be confined by his or her influences, whether biological or environmental. Preferably, a human is structured to be actively involved in the designing and actualization of his or her desired reality or destiny, as many would like to call it. This, believe it or not, starts in the brain or just the thoughts of an individual.

To back this statement is a quote from Buddha that states, "We are what we think". This statement means that our actions are dependent on our thoughts - the core of cognitive behavioral therapy. For one to understand what emotions he or she has to a particular event, it is essential

First to discover what he or she thinks about that event or radically the meanings he or she attaches to what is happening. It may not seem that important, but people are usually different.

For example, a person who has lost their job may find it hard to go on with life because of an increased burden on his or her shoulders, and thus may end up getting depressed. On the other hand, another person in the same situation may find this relieving. This is because maybe he or she did not find the working environment conducive. This person may even adopt a celebratory mood. Can you see the difference in response to the same situation?

The one thing that one notices from the above example is that the effect of an event can simply be changed by the way we think about it. That is why you'll need guidance through CT (cognitive therapy). Cognitive therapy gives one a wide variety of ways to think about what is affecting them. Even in the worst of cases, one will have several viewpoints on how one can view the situation. It is like when a person dies and the bereaved, instead of mourning the deceased death, start praising him or even celebrate a life well lived.

How many of us do that?

Information processing becomes distorted when we experience emotional distress

To start with, what is the meaning of emotional distress? It is an unpleasant feeling that usually affects our thinking. Anxiety, stress, and depression are all types of emotional distresses. These distress forms are normal to human beings.

However, they can become problematic when one cannot manage his or her feelings, and this can lead to cognitive lapses. That is where cognitive therapy comes in handy. CT is usually based on an information-processing model that merely depicts the fact that when one is going through some emotional distress, he or she tends to overthink events or, in short, one's judgment becomes distorted.

A good example is when one is about to go to a job interview, he or she tends to accumulate a lot of stress and anxiety on whether they will get the job. This kind of emotional distress can cause one not to be attentive to the interviewers, or may lead one to not answer questions correctly.

Some may ask how emotional distresses affect our thoughts and decisions. This is a relatively simple question to answer. The psychological state of a person can change his or her brain in many ways. The first way is by altering the hormones and neurotransmitters that we rely on to think. These can be modified negatively, making one not think clearly. The second way is through sleep, fatigue, and maybe even headaches. However, this is usually indirect on the latter.

Dangerous as it may seem, one can be taught how to manage his or her distresses. The primary way to do this is by undergoing cognitive therapy. CT teaches clients first to identify and correct errors associated with these types of judgments. Other recommendable ways to manage these feelings include spending more time with loved ones, indulging in exercises, or having a proper diet every day.

CHAPTER 1 - UNDERSTANDING CBT

Cognitive behavioral therapy is not something that you try on yourself. It's just not going to happen. You have to work with a trained therapist or counselor. While you do the heavy lifting as far as your personal beliefs and your responses to the outside world go, you need expert guidance. You need somebody who knows what they're doing and who knows what to instruct you. They must have been around the block a few times so they know what to anticipate.

This is a one common misconception about cognitive behavioral therapy or CBT for short. A lot of people think that if they just read a book on CBT, they would know the ins and outs of this alternative therapy system, and they can pretty much treat themselves.

There's more to recovery through CBT than just buying a book and learning techniques. You have to actually put them to use. This is the difficult part. You have to keep using these techniques no matter how inconvenient they can be. You have to keep practicing them no matter how busy you get.

Given these logistical considerations, it's no surprise that a lot of people think that you need specially trained counselors or psychiatrists to go through a CBT program. Most of the time, the main value these professionals bring to the table is they give you a formal structure for CBT. You can still do it yourself- you just have to give yourself the time, the space, and you need to commit to doing CBT consistently.

It's very hard to get out from under your mental habits if you are trying to do CBT alone. You need to be under the proper guidance of an experienced therapist who not only understands how it works and how its principles can be tweaked to apply your personal situation but who also knows how to measure success.

You have to understand that this is a results-based therapy. You don't just undergo CBT because you're just trying to "feel better". Who knows what that means? It's too subjective.

When you're working with a trained cognitive behavioral therapist, you are made aware of how your interpretations of things happening in your life impact your feelings, your interpretation of reality and, ultimately, your behavior.

The main goal of cognitive behavioral therapy is not just to feel good or feel at peace. Medication can do that. Being with the right people can do that.

Instead, CBT aims for something higher. It seeks to teach you how to effectively interpret life in such a way that you remain positive, empowered and in control. In other words, with the proper guidance, CBT would help you handle your life in a very different way.

People who normally seek cognitive behavioral therapy feel that their life is spiraling out of their control. They feel that they're stuck. It's as if they're watching a movie of their life, and they really can't do anything about it except just sit back and let things happen.

Properly implemented, cognitive behavioral therapy enables you to reclaim your personal power over your life. Believe it or not everything that happens in your life is your responsibility ultimately. A lot of people try to run away from this truth. In fact, to a lot of people, this is quite inconvenient and uncomfortable.

Unfortunately, regardless of how we feel, the truth is still the truth. We are always in control of how we respond to the world and this response is never neutral. It always has an impact on what we feel and, ultimately, what we do.

Cognitive behavioral therapy focuses on how people make sense of their world in terms of their interpretation. This is the foundation of cognitive behavioral therapy.

When you change the interpretation, you change how people emotionally respond to things, and this can lead to a profound impact on how they do things.

For example, somebody who is suffering from low self-esteem issues usually looks at any situation from a perspective of doubt. They don't think they're good enough. They don't think they're good-looking enough. They don't think people would like them. They don't think they would belong, so on and so forth.

Since this is how they interpret the signals people and situations give them, it is no surprise that they tend to miss out on opportunities or avoid social settings. They doubt themselves so much. They feel that people would not like them. They feel uncomfortable.

This is not just happening in their heads because when somebody has such a low self-esteem, and they're doubting themselves all the time, this can have physical effects... You can physically feel like you're about to throw up. You feel like you're shaking. You want to curl up into a ball or assume the fetal position.

Unfortunately, people with low self-esteem think that this is natural. They've responded to the world this way for so long they think that it's part of them. Some even say it's just who they are. It’s port of their personality. No, it's not.

Cognitive behavioral therapy goes to the root of the problem. The root of the problem is not that feel that you're ugly or that you assume that you are going to screw things up the moment you are given any kind of responsibility.

Instead, it goes straight to the issue - your low self-esteem. Why is that? Why do you automatically feel that people are not going to like you? Why do you automatically fear social settings or any kind of opportunity you learn? How are you looking at your situation? Are there any alternative interpretations?

A crucial part of CBT beat is the identification of negative thought patterns. They have to be clear about their thought process.

CBT doesn't assume that there's something wrong with you. Instead, you are first walked through the process of clearly describing how you view yourself, how you interpret reality and how you find yourself in certain situations.

There's no right or wrong answer here. The focus is objective truth. In other words, it's all about accuracy.

The next step is to look at the thought patterns involved and understand that it’s just one possible train of thought.

For example, if you go into a bar and you see a very attractive member of the opposite sex turn around, look at you and laugh. If you have a low self-esteem, you would automatically assume that person is laughing at you. Are there alternative interpretations?

A CBT therapist will step you through the alternatives and help you process that memory in such a way that it doesn't lead to negative thoughts and, ultimately, negative actions.

Maybe in that memory there was somebody cracking a joke behind you or making some faces. Perhaps that good-looking person was looking at that person behind you. It doesn't have to be you.

As long as the alternative interpretation are supported by facts, the CBT therapist can help you come up with a healthier approach to processing social information so you get out from under your social phobia.

Speaking of phobias, CBT is quite effective in this field. Take the case of an individual with dental phobia. This person is just deathly afraid of visiting the dentist. We’re not just talking about root canal here. We’re talking about just regular cleaning.

A CBT practitioner would ask this person about their past experience going to the dentist. The patient would then go through story after story until they get to the traumatic incident that led to an unhealthy association of the dentist with pain. It may have happened when the patient was five years old.

The therapist would then work with the patient to cut that mental connection between dentist and pain. In other words, they help the person realize that what happened in the past can stay in the past. Just because they had a traumatic experience that one time doesn't necessarily mean that all people going to dentists always suffer the same experience. They may just have been unlucky that day.

Oftentimes, the further we are from the memory, the more we blow it out of proportion. We exaggerate. It may turn out that when the patient was a kid, they just experienced slight pain, but as they got older, they remember the pain as something far worse.

An expert cognitive behavioral therapist can help patients go through this process successfully.

Understanding Anxiety and Depression

Experiencing intermittent anxiety is common and a normal part of life. Nevertheless, individuals with anxiety disorders often have excessive, intense, and persistent fear and worry about everyday circumstances and events. Usually, anxiety disorders involve recurrent episodes of unexpected feelings of intense fear, terror, and nervousness that reach the peak within minutes, also known as panic attacks.

Warning Signs and Symptoms of Anxiety and Depression

You may pinpoint the cause and origin of depression if it is tied to a life event, for instance, the death of a loved one, end of a relationship, or job loss. Sometimes we feel depressed and cannot identify a clear reason. Either way, symptoms and signs of depression ought to be taken seriously.

The symptoms of depression may vary in different people. We will many different types of depression with some being more serious and severe than others. We will look at the symptoms of common depressions that affect a larger population.

Major depression can be devastating. Some individuals have a single major depressive episode while others may have several. Major depression may last for two weeks or more. The main symptoms of major depression include:

- Low mood
- Suicidal thoughts or attempts
- Loss of energy
- Poor concentration
- Loss of interest in life
- Appetite and weight changes
- Hard time making decisions
- Insomnia or sleeping excessively

Major depressive disorder can also happen without an apparent reason. It may be brought on by events like:

- Death of a loved one
- Illness
- Divorce
- Other influential life changes

If one suffers major depression, they may feel like life is no longer meaningful or worth living. It is hard to envision life being any better. That is the mental disorder talking. [IMPORTANT] The person must seek depression treatment to get a reprieve from severe depression symptoms.

Persistent depression disorder (PDD) is less severe than the major depression, but they do share some symptoms. Individuals with PDD suffer low mood for two years or longer. PDD is at times referred to as a high-functioning depression. Friends and family may not guess that one is struggling with this disorder because they seem to do fine at school or work. One may be sad, tired, and feel bad about himself most of the time. Individuals with PDD are likely to have major depression episodes. Some research indicates that approximately 75 percent of people with PDD have struggled with major depression occasionally.

Seasonal affective disorder (SAD) occurs at specific times of the year. One is likely to fall into depression symptoms during winter when the days are shorter and typically end in the spring. Most of the affected persons have mild symptoms while others experience symptoms that are likely to make them withdraw. SAD symptoms may include:

- Low energy

- Isolation
- Sleep issues
- Carbohydrate cravings
- Overeating and weight gain

Situational depression, well-known as an adjustment disorder, stems from issues and problems with a certain situation. One can easily identify why they are depressed. Some of the issues that may lead or contribute to situational depression include:

- Divorce
- Involvement in an accident
- Death of a loved one
- Developing a serious illness
- Involvement in a crime

In some scenarios, situational depression may develop into major depression. Hence, it's advisable to speak out or see a mental health professional to ensure symptoms do not worsen.

Bipolar disorder, also known as manic depression, is a mood disorder. People experiencing this depression have mood swings that revolve around extreme lows and extreme highs. These cycles are called depressive episodes and manic episodes. The time taken between the mood shifts may vary from a few times in a year to several times in a week. Manic episodes may feel exhilarating while bipolar depression may feel very dark. One is likely to enjoy the manic episodes but may dread the depression episodes. This depression is a disruptive and troublesome condition that causes significant problems in an individual's life and their relationships. They should have behavioral therapy to manage the bipolar symptoms.

Atypical depression is characterized by uncommon and unpredictable depression symptom patterns, and it can last for two weeks or more. One may feel sad most of the time though certain events and circumstances may lift their mood. An individual may also feel some physical symptoms which may include:

- Fatigue
- Low mood that is lifted with some good news or positive external events
- A feeling of physical heaviness in your body
- Weight gain or appetite increase

- Extreme sensitivity to rejection
- Sleeping more but still feeling tired

Premenstrual dysphoric disorder (PMDD) may affect some women, causing them to suffer depression symptoms during their period. The depression is more disruptive than what most people think of as PMS. The symptoms of PMDD include:

- Mood swings
- Hopelessness
- Difficulty concentrating
- Self-criticism
- Tiredness
- Severe anxiety or stress
- Food cravings and binges
- Crying spells
- Irritability
- Body aches

If you frequently struggle with some of these common symptoms of depression, you need behavioral therapy and, if necessary, may need to check in with a mental health professional for further help.

For anxiety, the symptoms are more of the same. We have listed them below. The same symptoms might still be seen in other forms of depressions not discussed above. These symptoms may include:

- Feelings of sadness, emptiness, despair, and hopelessness
- Irritability and guilt
- Loss of interest in previously enjoyable activities
- Feelings of severe tiredness and exhaustion
- Poor concentrate or memory loss
- Attempts of suicide or suicidal thoughts
- Disinterest in relationships and daily activities
- Changes in appetite
- Insomnia, sleeping too much or too little
- Feeling out of control

- Lack of energy
- Feelings of tearfulness and mood swings
- Feelings of tension
- Feeling, agitated, irritable, or angry because of trivial inconveniences or for no reason.
- Feelings of worthlessness
- Restlessness
- Pains and aches without a medical condition

Causes of Depression

Experts do not believe there is one cause of depression, but it involves several external and internal factors. Most people possess a genetic predisposition to depression, i.e., internal. At times that could be adequate to cause intense depressive symptoms with certain circumstances. Sometimes external factors stimulate depressive symptoms. These external factors are likely to lead to depression in individuals who do not possess any genetic predisposition. The external factors may include:

- Chronic illness
- Traumatic events, e.g., rape, violence, and natural disaster
- Complex trauma, often resulting from childhood abuse or neglect
- Conditions that can lead to shake off the brain's balance of norepinephrine and serotonin, e.g., substance abuse, eating disorder, compulsive gambling, compulsive sexual behaviors, etc.

There are a multitude of psychological, genetic, social, and hormonal factors that come into play when referring to the causes of depression in human beings.

Biology and Hormones

Biologically speaking, it is indicated that depression runs in the blood of families with evidence that there are some genetic makeups prone to depression while some genetic makeups are more resistant to it.

Psychological Causes

When it comes to psychological causes of depression, women are more prone to them than men. Women are more likely to harbor and rehash negative feelings during bouts of depression as compared to men, who tend to be more emotional.

Social Causes

Choice of relationships, coping skills, and lifestyle decisions affect people differently. People are likely to suffer depression from relationship or marital problems, work-life balance issues, stressful life events, and financial troubles. Stressful events in life take part in developing and leading an individual to being depressed. Ongoing conflicts between individuals or groups affect our well-being, just like environmental and social stressors. These social stressors can be financial difficulties, unemployment, retirement, loneliness, childbirth, or loss of something important or someone. In vulnerable individuals, these unkind life events may be adequate to worsen a depressive disorder. An individual's personality characteristics are a significant factor. When human beings get depressed, they habitually view themselves and the world very negatively. We tend to not appreciate the good things, and the bad things overwhelm us. Some individuals view things in this manner even when they aren't depressed. This means they may have a depressive personality style.

The other possible cause of anxiety and depression is medications or physical illness. Hepatitis, glandular fever, alcohol and other substances of abuse, diabetes, influenza, thyroid hormones, birth control pills, anemia, and other medications like those for treating blood pressure or heart conditions may all bring about symptoms of depression.

The other conditions that have been proven to bring about depression include conditions such as strokes, HIV/AIDS, Parkinson's disease, and diabetes among others.

CHAPTER 2 - INTRUSIVE THOUGHTS AND GOAL SETTING

CBT is based on the premise that it isn't the situation or circumstances that cause the condition, but the meaning assigned to these situations that lead us to experience depression or anxiety. The way we interpret a particular situation is what makes us slip into a negative state of mind. Often, the ideas that we hold about events or situations are impractical or blown out of proportion.

When these misleading notions are not challenged, they continue to grow stronger and lead to even more negativity. We assume it as our reality, which blocks us from perceiving things as they are and leading a fulfilling life. There is a tendency to overlook or ignore things that do not match our negative perception of events and situations. We continue to let these thoughts grow unhindered.

For instance, a person suffering from depression will think that he/she just can't go to the office today because nothing's going to be positive. Their thoughts operate from a sense of hopelessness. They end up believing what they think is true. So according to the person, nothing positive is bound to happen at work today, which means with their negative thought pattern there's absolutely no opportunity of knowing if this feeling is right or wrong. The person doesn't give himself/herself a chance to ascertain the veracity of their claims. Their thinking itself leads to the negative or unpleasant experience.

In the above example, the person stays at home and doesn't go to work. Thus he/she doesn't know whether their negative prediction had any clear basis. Such individuals sit at home thinking that they are an absolute failure and that they've let people down. They become angry with themselves and think about how incompetent and useless they are. This leads to the person feeling even worse than earlier, which results in more difficulty while attending office the following day. This causes a downward thinking, behavior and feeling spiral or a vicious circle that leads to several problems.

Where Do The Thoughts Originate?

According to the founder of CBT Aron Beck, the thoughts can be traced back to our childhood, when they become relatively rigid and involuntary. For instance, a child who may not have got enough attention and affection from the family but was encouraged to perform well academically may grow up with the notion that people have to be a success or do well every time. Such individuals will start believing that if they are not successful, people won't accept them. This may lead to the person putting excessive pressure on himself and slipping into depression if he fails to meet their own standards for success.

They may not experience the desired success due to something that's beyond their realm of control, which triggers the negative or dysfunctional thought. The person may believe that he/she isn't good enough or is a total failure. This will lead them to think they won't be accepted by others, and hence withdraw socially.

Cognitive behavioral therapy helps people to gain awareness of the fact that their mind is processing thoughts in a more skewed manner. It assists them in stepping out of their involuntary thought pattern and challenges these unfounded thoughts.

In the above instance, it challenges the person to assess her real-life instances for determining whether her thoughts are in congruence with reality. If something that has happened in their past or to someone else has indeed matched their perspective about the situation.

This helps them gain a greater realistic perspective, and they may end up gaining an opportunity to test the perspectives of other people by revealing their situation to close friends and family members.

There's no denying that negative things happen. However, when we are in a tough state of mind, our perspective and interpretations operate from a more biased plane. Thus we magnify the challenge we face. CBT assists people in modifying these skewed interpretations and helps them see things from a more balanced perspective.

CBT for Intrusive OCD Thoughts

Cognitive behavioral therapy points out that OCD or Obsessive Compulsive Disorder is when people misread intrusive thoughts or compelling urges as indications that harm will occur and they are directly responsible for their actions.

When it comes to treating OCD or intrusive thoughts through CBT, it helps individuals understand that their intrusive or disturbing obsessive thoughts are nothing but a result of anxiety than any real danger. OCD patients are gradually made to realize that they won't be affected or in danger if they don't give in to these thoughts.

People with OCD are desperately trying to avoid harm. Their solutions invariably end up becoming part of the issue. For instance, if you keep thinking about neutralizing your thoughts about stabbing someone, it only ends up increasing these intrusive thoughts.

The real issues, therefore, aren't these intrusive thoughts but the meaning assigned to them by an individual suffering from OCD. For example, you may experience a huge urge to act upon your intrusive thoughts or that you shouldn't have these thoughts in the first place. This places a huge level of threat, anxiety, and responsibility on you. In the above example, you'll stop meeting the person alone or stop stocking your kitchen with knives. You've succumbed to the fear. The fear is still alive, and further stops you from thinking that your fear is nothing but a skewed thought.

One of the most important aspects of using CBT to treat OCD or intrusive thoughts is that the therapist only functions as a facilitator and that it has to be practiced on your own.

Different therapists focus on different cognitive and behavioral attributes of OCD or intrusive thoughts. A cognitive focused approach will help you assess your thought patterns more keenly. For instance, you have thoughts about killing someone, which makes you feel that are a bad person for having these thoughts and you could act upon them. Your therapist will work with you to seek a different understanding of these distorted thoughts and give you an alternate technique for reacting to them.

If it's a more behavioral focused approach, it could be focused on educating yourself about how anxiety is felt by the body. It is about facing your fears and gradually taking on, and increasing the very activities you fear. For instance, if you suffer from social anxiety, your therapist will slowly get you to come out of your shell and participate in interactions on a smaller scale.

Where OCD or intrusive thoughts are concerned, the end goal of CBT is to change the brain's thought process or structure. Even if this sounds like a Herculean task, it isn't. Let's consider an example.

Let's assume you have lived in the United States of America all your life, and are used to a right-hand drive. There was no hassle of changing gears. Suddenly, you have to move to the United Kingdom, which is a left-hand drive. How will you manage?

To learn to drive left-handed, you have to unlearn right-handed driving. What makes the entire pursuit tough is that it has become a subconscious or almost involuntary process. If you've never driven left-handed, you'll initially have trouble getting used to sides, looking in the wrong direction and stepping out.

However, once you change or alter your actions and gradually get used to driving left-handed, you will learn to drive in the new direction. It comes with exposure, practice, and repetition. Repeated left handed driving experiences help you navigate corners, look in the right direction and step out with confidence. You practice this repeatedly until you've altered your brain structure.

Similarly, CBT seeks to question the veracity of your intrusive thoughts by consistent action, thus leading to a change in thought patterns. It transforms unrealistic and impractical intrusive thoughts into more real and evidence focused patterns. CBT will also help you restructure your behavior about avoiding certain things that lead to intrusive thoughts. For instance, if you experience repetitive thoughts about wanting to stab someone, you overcome avoiding holding knives or being alone with the person. Over a period of time, repeated new experiences help your brain learn to control anxiety experienced as a result of these irrational thoughts.

Setting Your Goal and Getting Started

Why Set Goals?

Goal setting is a fantastic form of self-motivation. When you set goals, you give yourself something to strive for. You have something you know you want and you are able to identify that in order to have a clear idea of what your actions are for. These goals can be anything, from getting a new job to learning a skill or meeting new people. Literally, anything you would like to achieve in life can be made into a goal. Just because anything can be made into a goal does not mean that there are no guidelines, however. By following some rules, and guidelines when setting your goals, you will learn to come up with goals that will be beneficial for you and help you change your behavior or life for the better. Ultimately, your goal should offer you some sort of benefit, whether

Bad Goals

Before getting into what rules there are to rule-setting, let's first analyze what makes a goal bad. There are three types of goals you should seek to avoid, as they are not conducive to a healthy mindset, nor are they effective for the right reasons. These goals are goals seeking to be in certain emotional states, goals that focus on the past, or goals that are rooted in negativity. Each of these types of goals is poorly formed or unproductive for various reasons.

Emotional States

Oftentimes, when people are setting goals for therapy, they think, "I want to feel happy in my own body and mind." At face value, this is a fine goal, but in reality, it is deeply rooted in feelings. However, feelings are constantly changing and fluctuating. This means that your goal may be achieved some of the time, but no one is every happy with themselves all of the time. You cannot help that sometimes; you will be disappointed or angry in yourself for something you did or a way you behaved. Because of the instability of emotions, they should be avoided as goals.

Focus on the past

People frequently also decide to set their goals as, "I want to get back to my old self," especially if their symptoms they are hoping to fix came up later in life. It is not unusual to miss the person you used to be but remember, that person is in the past. That person you used to do not go through the hard times you are hoping to get yourself out of, nor did that person have the knowledge you do now. CBT seeks to focus on the present and fix your mental health issues through actions, not by seeking out the past. The past can never be made present again, and you should never try to root your goals in returning to a past relationship, a past personality, or past feelings. You will always fail.

Negative or avoidant goals

Just as affirmations have to be kept positive in order to be effective, so too do goals. While the goal of, "I want to avoid feeling depressed," might sound like a reasonable goal, all this is doing is making you hyper-focused on avoiding the feelings of depression. By focusing on avoiding rather than on fixing the distressing symptoms, you are running from your problem. You also set yourself up for failure, because any time you fail and feel depressed, you will feel that depression compound onto itself as you collect another piece of evidence that you are as worthless and helpless as you thought you were. Ultimately, it is best to avoid setting goals with a focus on negativity or avoidance and instead focus on goals that are active instead.

SMART Goals

Now that you understand what not to do with your goals, it is time to learn what good goals consist of. It helps to remember that SMART goals are the most effective goals, with SMART being an acronym for specific, measurable, attainable, relevant, and timely. If you remember this acronym, you will be able to make your goals work for you.

Specific

When setting your goal, you want to be as specific with what you wish to attain as possible. The more specific you are, the clearer the picture you paint in your mind of what you want to achieve. There is a huge difference between saying you want to paint your room blue instead of specifying that you specifically want a light cerulean color, and likewise, there is a difference between saying you want to manage feelings of anger and angry outbursts, and stating that you want to reduce your outbursts over the course of the month. You went from a somewhat specific goal to one that gave an exact picture of what it will be.

Measurable

Just as more specific goals are desirable, having goals that are easily measurable is also crucial to set a good, productive goal. You need to be able to quantify what success looks like so you know exactly when you reach it, whether that is stating that you will write a certain amount of words a day, or save a certain amount of money. In the example of wanting to reduce anger outbursts, you could specify that you want to reduce the total number of times you react in anger by 40%. This goal now has a quantifiable definition of success.

Attainable

Your goal needs to be something you can actually reasonably complete. The easiest way to do this is to make sure your goal can easily be broken down into smaller goals to keep you motivated and moving forward. Every time you meet a goal, you feel encouraged, which keeps you moving forward, striving to complete more of your goals. This positive feedback loop reinforces the idea of meeting your goals, motivating you to start in the first place once your body and mind realize that doing so can be both beneficial and enjoyable. For example, if you set a goal of reducing angry outbursts, specifying smaller goals may make it more realistic for you to complete. You could say that you want to make it a point to have one less angry outburst than you did the day before every day. This gives you small milestone goals that will help keep you on track to attaining the whole goal.

Realistic

By making sure your goal is realistic, you avoid setting yourself up for failure. A realistic goal for one person is not going to be the same as a realistic goal for another; a fit, experienced mountain climber may be able to set and achieve a goal of climbing a huge mountain with a month to prepare, but the vast majority of people who do not mountain climb on a regular basis would likely find themselves falling out. Likewise, it can be realistic for one person to go running every day, but someone paralyzed from the neck down will never be able to attain it. Make sure your goal is reasonable and realistic to your specific situation. If you want to alleviate your anger issues and stop having angry outbursts, you have to set a realistic goal that recognizes that the process of changing your habits and mindsets.

Timed

Defining how long your goal will take gives you a clear goal with an end in sight. You give yourself a time to complete the goal by, and anything beyond that is deemed a failure. Keep in mind that you should give yourself a reasonable amount of time to complete your goal. Be realistic about your timeline and make sure it has at least some leeway for you to complete it while still giving yourself time as a motivator to work toward it. For example, if you want to reduce your angry outbursts, you decide on one month for the timeline to begin to see a reduction of 30%.

Examples of Goals

With an understanding of what a goal needs to be SMART, you will be ready to set goals that are beneficial to your mental wellbeing. Here are a few examples of goals. Try to identify whether they are SMART and if they are not, fix them to make them SMART.

- I will pass my class this quarter with at least a B average.
- I will exercise three days a week so I can lose five lbs. before summer
- I will read more.
- I will get a new job.
- I will save 10% of my paychecks every week, so I can buy a car by December.
- I will cut how often I have panic attacks in half by February.

CHAPTER 3 - BREAK NEGATIVE THOUGHTS

There has been much study on cognitive distortions, the inaccurate and harmful thinking patterns that lead to negativity and unhappiness. While we categorize sixteen types of distorted thinking, as written about by one of the leaders in cognitive behavioral therapy, some people have estimated that there can be up to fifty types of cognitive distortions. Yet, it can be quite difficult to make a complete list of these distortions, as many of them overlap with each other. For instance, both catastrophic and jumping to conclusions involves a person magnifying a problem unnecessarily.

Let's look at an example to understand how these cognitive distortions can overlap fully. Imagine an anxious and shy adult who is generally uncomfortable around people. They are beginning a new job, but this job entails interacting with not only new coworkers but customers, as well. This person may think:

"If I interact with people they may think I'm incompetent and laugh behind my back. I will be too humiliated to continue working, and then I'll be fired and won't be able to pay my bills."

This person is thinking on an emotional level. They are anxious about their social interactions and competence level, which leads them to emotionally reason that people will laugh behind their back. They then begin to jump to conclusions, magnify, and catastrophize the situation, believing that they will be humiliated and unable to show their face. This fear then leads to them believing that they will be out of a job and unable to keep up with their bill payments.

These fears also illustrate black and white thinking, where the person believes the experience will be all bad with no room for good outcomes. They are also struggling with the fortune telling distortion by trying to assume what will happen with little evidence.

But, the primary distortion they are struggling with is emotional reasoning, as many of the unsupported and inaccurate negative thoughts arise from feelings of extreme anxiety.

With all of these cognitive distortions arising from negative emotions and thoughts, what can be done to help sort through it and take a step back? There's no one simple way out of this negativity; after all, it is easy to fall into self-sabotaging thought patterns. But, if you use cognitive behavioral therapy tools and approaches consistently on a regular basis then you will find that before long your thought patterns change and it becomes easier. It isn't easy to challenge your own thought processes and habits. Yet, if you practice doing this time and again then you will achieve the success you desire. You will find yourself with a new healthier thought process that isn't based in negativity, fear, and anxieties.

This progress can be achieved as cognitive behavioral therapy is based in providing people with a way to gain internal distance from their negative thoughts and emotions so that they can better analyze them, understand which thoughts are distorted, and then challenge these distortions. With CBT you can learn to replace a negative, emotion-fueled, and impulsive thought with one that is more rational, balanced, and true. After developing a habit of testing which thoughts are true and which are false you will more easily understand the validity of your thoughts without much conscious effort.

Imagine again our anxious person who is starting a new job. If they are able to learn tools to take a step back from their negative thought patterns and anxieties, then they may be able to challenge their irrational beliefs.

By confronting their anxiety and negative thoughts with clear, balanced, and truthful statements and questions that have supporting evidence they can overturn the negativity and see that there is nothing but lies behind the fear. Once the negativity is revealed to have no basis, then it has no hold on the person and they can feel confident in the truth that they have discovered.

Are they really incompetent? Why would people think that they are incompetent? Even if they make a mistake, would everyone really laugh at them? Are these expectations accurate? No, they aren't. Upon realizing this, the person may think:

"At my previous jobs, even if I made a mistake people didn't laugh at me. People haven't acted as if I'm incompetent. In fact, I can usually do my work without attracting any negative attention."

As the person begins to unravel the lies and see the truth they will be able to continue making more true statements which support that they have nothing to be afraid of. These statements prove that the negative thoughts and anxieties have no base in reality, and therefore there is no reason to be afraid.

Along with challenging the likelihood of being incompetent and laughed at, the person may also choose to test the validity of their fears. They might accept that even if they aren't laughed at out loud, that they may still feel embarrassed and self-conscious while at work. In this case, they can challenge the embarrassment expectations. How can they do this? By telling themselves that it doesn't matter.

Of course, simply saying "it doesn't matter," won't help anyone feel better. This is why they must follow it up with an accurate and true assessment of if the job will actually lead to them feeling constant self-conscious and embarrassed. They might remind themselves that their jobs have made them feel self-conscious at times in the past, but it wasn't all bad. These feelings didn't prevent them from making friends with coworkers and competently handling their job. The person might remind themselves they've been embarrassed at work before, but it didn't stop them from going to their job on a daily basis, and it didn't lead to them feeling embarrassed on a daily basis. They were still able to find ways to enjoy parts of their job and do what was expected of them.

With rational and balanced statements such as these, the person may be able to challenge the idea that any embarrassment will be nearly as bad as their perceive. They can realize that even if they do become embarrassed, it won't lead to any long-lasting consequences. By reminding themselves that it doesn't matter if something embarrassing happens, they can realize that while sometimes difficult situations do occur, the resulting outcome is rarely as catastrophic as we imagine.

We all struggle with cognitive distortions, sometimes on a daily basis. Just as the human brain can think with clear fact-based logic, it can also think in an emotionally-driven cycle with little to no evidence to back up its fears. But, by finding the strength to challenge your own negative thoughts, you can overturn harmful thought patterns and replace them with healthy thinking.

By learning to adopt healthier thinking patterns you can learn to which thoughts of yours are helpful and which are unhelpful. This, in turn, can help you know how they affect your feelings and how you respond to problems that might be troubling you. With regular practice, you can learn to adopt helpful and true thoughts in place of negative and anxiety-inducing thoughts which only serve to discourage you. As you are better able to stop negative thoughts, you will find that you are better at caring for yourself, helping others, and taking life's challenges as they come at you. Better yet, you will find that your mental health improves, helping you to reduce anxiety, manage depression, cope with stress, improve sleep, and better manage your body weight.

Healthy thinking and taking a step back to examine your negative emotions require you first to calm your mind and body. Cognitive behavioral therapy greatly focuses on techniques which can aid in this, such as yoga, meditation, mindfulness, journaling, muscle relaxation, and more. In order to fully practice CBT, you should use these methods and techniques on a daily basis, as this is how you will get to a place where healthy thinking becomes a natural thought process. Instead of focusing on the negative, you will find it natural to consider positive and neutral alternatives. With regular practice, negative thoughts and anxieties will no longer control your life or your mind.

Guesses Rather than Fact

Many people begin using cognitive behavioral therapy specifically to help them better manage and control their thoughts and emotions. Although, there are also many people who use this therapy to help control their addictions and other destructive behaviors and patterns. One of the most powerful ways to help people to learn to step back and control these thoughts is to treat their automatic thoughts as guesses rather than fact.

Living in the world, we all naturally have thoughts about our surroundings, ourselves, our various relationships, the past we have lived through, and the future we are preparing for. Having the ability to think such thoughts give us an understanding of the world around us and help us know how to respond to situations. It is this ability that allows us to create, solve problems, manage our day to day living, and improve our lives. But, just as these thoughts can be a powerful tool in helping us to excel, they can also be our downfall. If we live in negative thought patterns we can end up suffering, self-sabotaging, and creating more problems for ourselves.

This is especially common in people suffering from the emotional and mental strain from anxiety disorders, clinical depression, bipolar disorder, and other mental illnesses. Remember, there is nothing to be ashamed of if you have a mental illness, just as the flu or a broken leg is nothing to be ashamed of. But, sadly for people living with these conditions, they tend to get stuck in negative thought cycles which are pessimistic and get in the way of their daily lives. Frequently, people with anxiety disorders will catastrophic their situations, overestimating the danger or negative impact situations have had or might possibly have in the future.

As people with mental illnesses continue to have these thoughts they get sucked deeper and deeper into a cycle of pain and negativity, which becomes increasingly difficult to get out of. But, with CBT methods these people can slowly replace their negative thought processes with positive, pulling themselves out of the hole of pain and negativity. As time goes on and they continue to practice their new positive thought process will become second nature.

A common technique for negative thinking, especially in relation to "fortune telling," "jumping to conclusions," and "catastrophizing," is to treat your thoughts not as fact, but as guesses. This works because, the truth is, many of our thoughts are based on our feelings and pasts. This makes the thoughts simply conclusions we have come to, not accurate facts. As an example, if you are struggling with a specific new class in college, you may assume that it is too difficult and you simply are unable to succeed. This can lead to thought processes such as "I can't do this," leading you to give up.

But, if you take the thought that you are unable to succeed as a guess rather than a fact, then you are more likely to stick with the class and form an opinion after you have given it your all. Over time, you may find that you are much better at the class than you first expected. By treating this as a guess you don't become discouraged or overwhelmed, rather it is an opportunity to test out what you are good at.

Confusing thoughts and guesses with facts can be extremely damaging to your thought processes, self-esteem, and success. Keep in mind to always check your thoughts and don't automatically believe them to be true facts.

To begin thinking of your thoughts as guesses rather than fact try using alternative explanations. For instance, in the example above of someone who is struggling with a new college class, they may adjust their thinking to:

•"This is only the beginning of the class, with time and repetition it will likely get easier."

•"The class may be difficult because it is new and unfamiliar, making it appear more difficult than it actually is."

•"While the class may be difficult, that doesn't mean I am unable to learn. I will simply have to work harder than I first believed."

•"New subjects are often more difficult in the beginning. If I give it time, I can later on assess my ability after I have a better understanding of the subject."

•"Even if it is difficult and I can't do the class perfectly, it is worth the effort. There are reasons I need to learn this material, regardless of whether or not it is easy."

You will find that by learning to treat your automatic thoughts as only one possible guess rather than a fact it will help prevent you from rigidly holding onto a negative idea. This will help you to think more flexibly so that you can come up with more balanced and healthy perspectives. When you think flexibly with the ability to consider multiple possibilities you will find it easier to choose to consider the most effective idea. In this case, the more effective idea is that you should stick with the class and try it out rather than giving it up.

When you find yourself especially struggling, despite trying the above method, try one or more of the following techniques:

1.When you find yourself feeling strong negative emotions such as anxiety, anger, or sadness take a moment and stop. Identify the thoughts you are struggling with which seem to be most responsible for the strong emotions you are feeling.

2.Find the thought which seems to affect you the most. Remember, this thought s only one way of thinking about the available information, and it is not necessarily a fact.

3.Consider and many other possible hypotheses as you can, even if you don't believe them or think of them as fact. This will help you think more flexibly. Write these hypotheses down.

4.Choose a few hypotheses that appear the most helpful. Write down how you might act or feel differently if you adopt the hypotheses as fact.

5.After you analyze the most helpful hypotheses decide on which one is the most helpful once applied to your situation. After you have decided, continue to remind yourself of this thought as frequently you can on repeat. By doing this you can't expect the negative thoughts to disappear, but they will reduce and become less dominant. Over time, you will find that the new healthier thought takes hold and becomes easier to believe, positively affecting your feelings and behavior.

You may also find help in realizing that the negative thoughts are simply boring. This may not help everyone. But, consider your negative thoughts as an annoying acquaintance who is always coming to you to complain. You wouldn't put up with this person on a daily basis. You would get bored and tune them out or tell them to complain to someone else. The thing is, you can do the same with your negative thoughts.

Whenever you find yourself having repeated negative automatic thoughts simply tell yourself that it's annoying. You can roll your eyes, and say "oh, it's simply the same boring thoughts again." By doing this, you recognize that not all of these thoughts are important and that it's okay to let them go.

If you struggle with thoughts about what you should and shouldn't do, then you can learn to change your approach to these thoughts. This can be especially helpful if you are someone who struggles with addiction or procrastination.

For instance, the phrase "I should exercise," implies that you don't really want to follow through, that you are making yourself exercise. This may be true, but in order to change your behaviors you need first to change your thought process. Therefore, change what you tell yourself with something such as:

•It is important for me to stay healthy and exercise.

•It is best for me if I exercise

•I look forward to completing my exercise

•I like the way I feel after accomplishing my exercise.

While these expressions might feel hollow at first, you will find that with time they begin to ring true and your exercise becomes a new habit. It becomes not about what you should or shouldn't do, but about doing what is best for you in the long-run.

You can use this when you shouldn't do something, as well. For instance, instead of saying "I shouldn't drink," you can say:

- I choose not to drink.
- I am proud of myself for not drinking.
- I like the way I feel when I don't drink.
- Drinking is not a part of my life.

Using these methods and thought patterns you can take a step back and improve your thinking. By changing your thought patterns, you can then change your feelings and your actions. Before long, you will find it is much easier to step back from your negative thoughts and adopt new more positive and helpful thoughts in their place.

Obstacles and Bad Habits

What good are habits for battling negative mental states? In order for almost all of them to be successful, you need to ensure that you practice them regularly which means that your basic life habits are in order as well.

Furthermore, it turns out that simple things like eating better, exercising regularly and getting more sleep also make it easier to deal with whatever else is currently on your plate. With that in mind, this chapter looks at ways you can excise common bad habits so you can focus on what matters most.

Sleep better: Sleep does wonders for the human body, but too much or too little leaves us unable to think clearly. Our reaction time slows and our memory clouds. Which is to say nothing of the lack of energy that naturally results from too much or too little sleep. All these things drag us down and worsen anxiety. The cure is balance. Doctors recommend that adults get seven to nine hours of sleep a night. Of course, anxiety makes it difficult for us to sleep. Beyond using the exercises we've already gone over; better sleep helps you fight back. There are quite a few things you can do to achieve this end.

Loads of sleep studies have shown that when we use electronics can disrupt our sleep. The effects of light from monitors and television screens affect our bodies much longer than we'd normally think. A good sleep hygiene practice is to unplug from screen time an hour before bed. It may also improve your mood all around if you're an avid user of social media: studies have shown that those who use social media frequently feel more isolated, even in actual social settings. Your sleep may also improve simply because you'll be processing less information before hitting the hay. This is particularly true for news junkies.

To make good sleep habitual you need to set a schedule so your body knows what to expect when. The amount of sleep is just as important as when that sleep takes place. Set a specific time when you'll be in bed and when you'll get out of bed. The latter is easy: use an alarm. In time you'll wake up before the alarm even goes off. The latter can be harder to accommodate for depending on your living situation. But if you're willing to make the changes it will pay off. On a similar note, try spending less time when you're awake in your bed itself.

A strict sleeping schedule will allow you to be tired when you are supposed to and wake up feeling refreshed. You want to pick a time that you can have about nine hours of undisturbed sleep for example 10 pm to 7 am. You want 9 hours because it may take an hour for you to fall asleep. If anything comes up that is not urgent and involves you ruining your sleep schedule then decline it.

Some sleeping schedules may also be reversed and this can cause a lot of problems. The problems with this is that you will only be awake during nighttime and most people are awake in the daytime so you will not be able to make plans with your friends and other important things. Unless you have a job that requires you to work overnight shifts then you should try to fix your sleeping schedule immediately.

There are three different methods that work best for resetting your sleeping schedule these methods will also work if your sleeping pattern is just off by a few hours and you want a quick fix. The first method is to stay up until you are scheduled to sleep. This may be difficult because it involves you to be awake for over 24 hours, but if you can handle it then this is the fastest method.

The next method is also pretty difficult because it involves not getting adequate rest for one night and continuing throughout the whole day until you are scheduled to fall asleep. Basically how this works is that right before you fall asleep you want to set an alarm to wake you up in three or four hours. Once you wake up you must stay awake for at least 16 hours before you fall asleep. By doing this you are reversing your regular sleeping schedule by four or five hours and once you are on track you can start having a full night's sleep.

This last method takes the longest but it is also the easiest out of the three. It's easier than the other two methods because it doesn't require you to stay up for hours and hours with little sleep. To do this method you want to either try going to bed one or two hours earlier or later then what you are used to. So say for example you usually go to bed at 1 am and you wake up at about 9 am, and your goal is to be in bed by 8 pm and wake up at 5 am.

The first day you do this method you go to bed two hours earlier then what your used to so, in this case, it would be 11 pm. Then the next day it would be 9 pm. Then from here, you can just go to bed an hour earlier to make it 8 pm which is your goal. Depending on how far your original sleeping schedule is compared to your goal will determine how long this process may take.

Get more active: It's well known how physical activity relieves stress. But research has proven time and time again that exercise also battles anxiety the same way it battles depression. According to the Mayo Clinic, exercise releases endorphins to create a natural "high" of sorts. On top of this exercise signals the immune system to halt production of chemicals triggered by anxiety that worsen your symptoms. Though unproven, it's believed that the elevated body temperature resulting from a rigorous workout has a therapeutic effect on the nervous system. Regular exercise can improve your health all around.

But a lot of us simply don't like the idea of it, and that's a major hurdle. Whether it's the idea of gyms or feelings of inadequacy, we just don't want to get off our duffs and do something. This is where framing how we think comes in really handy. Exercise doesn't have to mean "exercise" with weights and machines. Exercise is merely a physical activity. Anything that you can do that gets you moving qualifies. Anything as simple as a walk around the block or a swim in the pool is enough. And if you frame it this way, it's easier to think of ways to incorporate other people into what you're doing, making it a social event, too, filling that emotional need.

If you live an inactive life style or have been inactive for a long period of time, you'll want to start small before going all out. Your end goal should be to engage in some form of physical activity every day, but when you start it's helpful to aim for every other day instead, just to get in the swing of it. It also isn't necessary to total exhaust yourself, either.

Your depth of sleep and amount of rest you get plays a role in the energy you have over the course of the day. The higher your level of physical activity, the better your sleep. When higher physical activity and better sleep are two goals you are working towards, the two will naturally complement each other, magnifying their benefits.

IF YOU HAVEN'T EXERCISED in a while you can consider the following a basic introduction to the types of exercises you can get started with in an easy and (relatively) painless fashion.

FIRST AND FOREMOST, however, it is important to keep in mind that everyone's body is different which means that what is right for you, might differ from what is suggested here. Have a clear idea of what your body is always trying to tell you, and never push yourself further than you feel comfortable with. It is always better to play it safe today, and train tomorrow then push too hard today and have to sit out for a week or more with a torn muscle instead.

IT IS important to always take the time to warm up before any strenuous activity as getting started directly without warming first is a great way to seriously hurt yourself in the process. Warming up properly will also help to raise your overall core temperature which helps make your muscle more elastic and more willing to benefits from the exercise you are doing. Additionally, taking the time to warm up properly will ensure that the maximum amount of blood flow is getting to and from the heart which will further help you successfully push your body to the limits. Regardless of the reasons, start every workout, no matter how minimal, with a good warmup first.

WHILE IT IS natural to want to always push yourself as hard as possible, in reality, a training regimen that involves alternating intensities is actually more effective in the long run. Not only will it help you to continue exercising regularly without injury, but the variation is also better when it comes to producing reliable muscle growth. Finally, it gives your body extra time to recover from the more intense workouts while not simply sitting around doing nothing. This means that your intense days can actually be more intense because you know you will have a rest before you have to do it all again.

JUST LIKE IT is important to always warm up before you exercise, it is equally important to take a few extra minutes at the end of your workout session to cool down properly with a little light cardio and some additional stretching. Not only will this prevent your muscles from cramping up on you later, but it will also actually help improve their growth because the cooldown ensures that they are receiving an appropriate amount of blood to maximize growth.

STARTING with basic yoga exercises is a great low-impact way to get started. As a physical practice, yoga can offer many benefits, and one of the best aspects of yoga as a physical practice is that there are variations of each pose that anyone can do.

IMPROVE YOUR EATING HABITS: We live in the golden age of convenience. It does make our lives easier—until it reaches our diet, that is. Grocery stores are brimming with pre-made meals and frozen dinners. Fast food restaurants are everywhere. When we're hungry it's easy to reach for one of these options and not think much of it. After all, they're quick and cheap most of the time. All the better! But what they say is true: we are what we eat. And what goes into those does more than curb our appetites.

Relax Your Mind and Decluttering Your Brain

Decluttering your mind must start with decluttering everything around you, and this means your space. That is the first step anyone should take. The process to clean and organize your things will help you make room in your mind for the things that really matter. Decluttering your home, your car, your desk – it is like therapy. By doing so, by going through all of your stuff, you will not only make some deep realizations about yourself, but you will see more clearly where your blocks really lay in life. This process of decluttering is the first step towards taking responsibility for your life and getting your hands dirty. Sometimes we think we know where our negative thoughts come from, but during this process, we become conscious of things that were blocked in our minds. These are things that were forgotten for a long time but still haven't really healed in our minds. I believe decluttering your living space is the first step towards a more minimalist mindset. A big plus of this process is that you get rid of your useless things. It is also a way to liberate more time for yourself and for your day-to-day life.

Start with small projects

Of course, you don't have to do it all at once. On the contrary, decluttering will teach you how to be more patient and more disciplined in your life. So, you can start little, especially if you tend to accumulate a lot. Don't be too hard on yourself. Identify certain spaces in your home or at the office that could be decluttered quickly. It could be your bathroom drawer or your bedroom nightstand. It could be the closet where you toss all your cables and electrical wares (I'm sure everyone has one of those). We usually tend to accumulate things in certain areas more than others. Starting small with an easy project will give you the momentum to pursue your decluttering and get rid of your useless stuff progressively.

It can be a vast process, and you might find it difficult to know where to start and the steps you'll need to go through to sort everything out. That's why it's so important to start with an easy project first. When you begin to make room in your space, you'll start to feel energized and enthusiastic almost immediately. Decluttering can be a funny process. For some people, it might be really exciting and exhilarating when they begin to get rid of their stuff. It can provide you a sense of control and freedom over your life rather instantly.

Take your time with big ones

First, think about what you want the result of this process to be. How does this reflect on your personality and who you are without the noise, without the stress, and without the limitations of time? You will discover yourself during your decluttering process and this will be the time to progress onto the bigger projects. As Marie Kondo explains [1], taking everything out of your closet spaces will help you understand the real weight of your stuff on your life. That's why it's important to take your time during this decluttering phases in order to deeply understand what you tend to accumulate and why. These realizations will free you, transform you, and help you understand yourself at a deeper level.

For example, for many people, one of the biggest challenges during decluttering is when it comes to their wardrobe. Removing everything out of your closet and putting it on your bed is a good way to sort everything out before putting some clothes back into your closet. With this process, you'll immediately feel what it's like to have an empty closet, and it's such an amazing feeling! Then, you can put back your favorite items and get rid of the rest in order to only keep the essentials, and the important pieces that you feel correspond to your own style and being.

Other big projects could involve cleaning your kitchen and pantry. You can have fun with this. You can find new ways to organize everything that will make it easier for you on a day-to-day basis. You can also identify areas where you're missing important things.

Another thing you could try is to buy clever appliances online that will help you organize your stuff in a more practical way. There are a lot of very clever items to help you out, especially on Amazon. You can find beautiful compartments for your kitchen, smart hangers for your closet, and so on. Remember that you are a minimalist now. So, do not misuse your cash on cheap and useless items. Think about the long-term, quality materials when purchasing and the items that you will really need.

Blocks and struggles that you might have

There are some projects that you may find more difficult to start. You may have similar struggles with what we call your "sentimental clutter." These are the relics from the past; the emotional items that make you travel back in time when you pull them out to look at them. These are often gifts from people you love but, realistically, you never use or have items of a similar nature. And in a way, I think it's beautiful that these items can make us feel a flow of emotions and nostalgia. But if we really think about it, it's not so much the things but the memories we attach to them that make us feel this way. Don't you feel the same emotions when you look at photos? Exactly. When I find it difficult to get rid of this emotional stuff, I just take a picture of the item so I can remember it forever. Then I pack it up carefully and just trash it (with dignity). Or you can donate it if the items are in good shape or of value. Maybe it can be useful to somebody else. The important thing is that you keep in mind that these things are just things, not the memories themselves. All of the good and bad memories are still with you, in your mind, and you can access them whenever you want to or you need to. That is your power here, and with it comes the confirmation that you don't need clutter in your life to remind you of something.

Bottom line - Liberate yourself from your physical clutter to access a clearer mind, free from the past and free to move forward.

How distractions pollute our thoughts

Too many distractions will clog your mind emotionally.

Distractions are everywhere. To name a few of the obvious distractions we have TV, Netflix, and the Internet. It's like everything is designed for our passive enjoyment, preferably from the comfort of our couch. Even if there is nothing wrong with these activities fundamentally, you will discover that they were not only taking up a lot of your time, but also preventing you from having more energy, more enthusiasm, and more focus. I'm sure you know this too, even if it's difficult to recognize the fact that we spend too much time on these activities. And also, because it's difficult to change, isn't it?

But decluttering your space can't be enough to clear your mind; you also need to declutter your time. Life is short, and you need to take action if you want to find focus and peace of mind.

The goal here is to find out where your time disappears and where you can declutter. All of us at least have the same amount of time in a day whether we are millionaires, CEOs, or geniuses. Everyone is completely equal to this simple fact. All of us have 24 hours on a daily basis to do what we want to do in our life. And if you're reading this, my bet is that you may not spend 100% of your day doing what you're meant to be doing, right? But no worries, awareness is always the first step towards progress and the important thing here is to become more conscious of yourself so that you can declutter gradually of the things that no longer serve you.

Small distractions are often what is keeping you from accomplishing the big things. Multitasking is really a myth. Studies have proven this over and over again. Doing many things at the same time doesn't help with concentration and, in the end, it doesn't provide the same kind of results. So, how can you concentrate on one thing at a time? How can you ignore every single distraction of every typical day? Have you heard of the Pomodoro technique? It's a really simple concept to help you focus at work and get more things done. The technique consists of concentrating on one task for a limited period of time: 25-minutes. Use a timer to monitor this time and avoid other distractions while working during this time. This way, the running of time gives you a sense of urgency, enabling you to focus more deeply on that amount of time. Between the phases of concentration, you can have 10-minute breaks to help you keep a natural rhythm.

New activities, new you!

Your habits make you who you are. So, if you want to change your life and change your mind, then you'll probably need to transform your habits completely. Making room for new habits is the first step. And this fresh, clean slate will allow you to add different and great activities that will feed your mind with positive and efficient thoughts. What is it that you have always wanted to try and never had the time to? Which activities are you secretly thinking about in the back of your mind? Is it singing or writing? It doesn't really matter, because you're free to do anything. And maybe if you finally try it, you won't like it, but so what? There is also a good chance you'll love it. So, trying new things is never a waste of time, and, in the end, you may find something you're passionate about, something you truly love. You'll also like the process of doing it on a very consistent basis, even when it's hard or inconvenient to do. You'll love it anyway. I can't advise you enough to find what it is that you love to do, so don't be afraid to try. You really have nothing to lose.

Maybe you know exactly which activities you'd like to invest yourself and your time into. But somehow you never found the time to act on it consistently. In this case, you need to define some goals. Nothing can be achieved without a real goal, a purpose, a mission, or a vision. Find what it is for yourself and define every step you need to take in order to reach it. Say that you always wanted to learn a foreign language. What does it really mean for you? How can you act on this goal every day, consistently? Maybe you could organize a training plan with lessons, live discussions with a coach, or, even better, a trip? Anyway, put it in your calendar so you can actively progress on it and achieve what you want. You need a vision if you want to focus on your life.

Bottom line is free yourself from distractions and from what consumes your time to find more freedom to do what you are meant to do.

CHAPTER 4 - KEEP CALM

Manage Excessive Anger

You don't have to try and sort out your anger management issues on your own. Counseling can help to get your mind straight, allow you to open up and set your issues free. There are group counseling sessions, private sessions and various clinics that can help you deal with your anger. It is up to you which you feel more comfortable with. There are hotlines set up that a person can call to find a doctor, therapists or groups in or around your area. The good thing about hotlines is that they are usually anonymous as is the internet where you can find a host of information on therapy centers, doctors and counseling groups as well.

There is no shame in getting help and it shows strength of character to make the move towards seeking it. It is not going to be easy but then again nothing worth fighting for ever is. Taking back control of your life and shaking the grips of anger management issues is worth that fight as it will completely turn your life around for the better.

Knowing When to Seek Help

Only you have the power to take back control of your anger and you do not have to do it alone. There are people and groups that can help guide you, support you and teach you how to manage your anger. If you feel you are out of control, get anxious about the things that trigger your anger and are abusive it is time to get help. Anger management issues have a negative impact on your life, relationships and health don't let it destroy you talk to a therapist or medical professional. There are also anger management classes where a person can get help and support, they need in group sessions.

Professional Therapy

An anger management therapist can help you establish an anger management program or let you know if you may need to take it one step further by seeking the advice of a psychiatrist for extra diagnosis. If your anger is driven by an underlying problem be it either a physical or mental health issue you will have to seek the diagnosis and help of a medical doctor. If the psychiatrist thinks you need to see various specialists, they will recommend you onwards to them.

What to Expect When Seeing a Professional Therapist or Medical Doctor

A professional therapist will if they think it necessary, send you to see a medical doctor/psychiatrist in order to properly diagnose any underlying emotional, physical or mental health issues that may be causing anger issues.

This is done by a series of tests that will differ depending on what the doctor is testing for and or the patient's age. Kids who experience anger issues may get a series of tests where they have to look at pictures, color, pick blocks of a swaying table and be tested in ways to find out if they have ADHD, ADD and so on. Adults will get tests according to their age group and what the doctor may think is the cause according to the symptoms described by either the patient, therapist or both. There may be a series of X-Rays and CT Scans to check for any injuries, lesions, etc.

Depending on the outcome of these tests the doctor may recommend that more medical attention might be required, prescribe various drugs such as an antidepressant, anxiety or mood stabilizing medication. Or they may just recommend anger management counseling.

Doctors do not really like to prescribe medication for anger control unless they feel the person has high levels of stress or anxiety that could be detrimental to their physical health. Not only do most of the drugs come with side effects such as a terrible thirst, headaches, nausea, and tremors they can also compound the anger management issues because they can become addictive. They can also alter a person's state of mind. People who have anger issues already battle with a loss of control and an altered state of mind.

Doctors will always recommend counseling or a wellness clinic before resorting to medication unless they feel the person is a risk to themselves and or others.

There are online tests that people can take to test to see if they have an underlying issue causing their anger and mood swings, but these is just an idea and they really should not be taken as a diagnosis. If you feel there is a lot more to your anger it is best to seek advice from a licensed therapist or medical professional.

If you have tried therapy and feel your issues getting worse go back to your doctor for advice maybe you need a different sort of counseling or they may need to run some more tests. The thing is not to give up if you feel you are not getting anywhere these things take time to build up and even more so to break down.

One on One Counseling

If you are not comfortable in a group therapy session, there is one on one counseling which can be done on site in the counselor's office or in this day and age you can have the session online. However, if you are going to opt for the online therapy sessions it may be prudent to actually meet and or check the therapist's credentials before committing to the therapy. One on one on-site counseling session lasts for around forty-five minutes to an hour. Therapy may last anywhere from a few weeks to months depending on the amount of therapy a person may require, and each case is different.

What to Expect When Attending One on One Counseling

One on one counseling is much the same as that of group counseling only you have the therapist's full attention. Each therapist will run the sessions in the way they see fit which most requires you to do all the talking. They will ask about various emotions, feelings, states of mind and various other questions pertaining to what was discussed during the session. It is much the same as going to see a psychologist/therapist because you have had a traumatic experience, feel you need to talk to someone, etc.

You will only get as much as you are willing to give out of each session and should go in there with an open mind. Relax as much as you can and remember they are not there to judge you but to listen, observe and guide you through your anger management therapy. The session is for you and all about you it will not help matters to go in there hot-headed and feeling insecure. The first session may be a bit awkward for you but as the therapy progresses you will start to relax into it to find that you are opening up more each time.

Do not expect it to work overnight and try as best you can to stick to your regular appointments. If you cannot make for whatever reason be sure to take a makeup session as each one is an important step in the process of learning to control your anger issues.

If you feel you are not comfortable or the right fit with your therapist be honest about it as you must feel you can trust and rely on them to help you through this tough time. But make sure that it is not just you are being defensive and insecure or feeling a bit vulnerable in the sessions rather than a clash with your therapist.

Be as open and honest as you can about what are feeling or going through you are only hurting yourself and slowing down your own recovery time by holding back in your one on one therapy sessions.

Your sessions may require you to go through a step by step program that your therapist will take you through and will require you to put in some extra work at home or at the office after the session is over. You will be required to attend sessions at least once a week for a designated amount of time the doctor or your therapist may think you require.

Maintain Mindfulness

What does the term mindfulness mean? Mindfulness is the quality or state of being conscious or aware of something. Mindfulness is a quality that everyone usually has. It is a quality that is always present to us in every moment. One only gets to realize it if you can take time to appreciate it. By practicing mindfulness, one also practices the art of creating space for ourselves and our reactions.

How can Mindfulness Help One in Overcoming their Challenges?

Mindfulness can be of importance in overcoming your challenges in that:

1.Mindfulness Gives One Perspective.

In times of anger, mindfulness can come in handy by giving you the ability to view a particular situation with a different perspective. One is therefore able to take a step back and make a sane decision devoid of any emotional judgment.

2.Mindfulness Leads You to Acceptance.

Many are the times when one wishes they could change a difficult situation they are maybe going through. This, however, is usually not possible. Mindfulness, in such a case, will teach you how to accept the outcome. It will also teach you that you may lack the power to change the circumstance, but you have all the power to change your attitude toward the circumstance.

3.Mindfulness Helps You Process Anger.

Often are the times in life when unfair circumstances are out of our control. This can cause anger which can lead to destruction of a lot of things in one's life. Mindfulness in this case will help one to understand their anger, rather than just express it. It will also teach one to respond to situations rather than just reacting to them.

4.Mindfulness Gives You Clarity.

This clarity is usually as a result of the perspective that mindfulness gives you. This is because when one removes the emotional judgment when dealing with a situation, one is able to have a clear view of what really happened. This, therefore, allows one to make informed and clear decisions on what to do next.

5.Mindfulness Helps You to Take Care of Yourself.

Mindfulness, as you may have noticed, involves meditation. It is this meditation that helps one understand their body's needs. Therefore, when one is faced with a particular situation, one is able to listen and act in accordance to their body's needs, and this leads to a self-care routine.

How Does One Maintain their Mindfulness?

Some people may find the art of mindfulness hard to comprehend. However, it is a very simple art that one can understand and maintain. Here are some tips that may help you maintain your mindfulness:

1.Practice Mindfulness during Routine Activities.

This tip might not seem that important to most people. However, it is one of the most helpful ways. On a daily basis, most people do not really put much concern on the daily routine activities that they undertake. These activities may include bathing, brushing teeth, or even taking breakfast. Bringing awareness, however, to these activities can help one maintain their mindfulness.

For example, one may try and focus on the way they breathe, their sight, or even their sense of smell. This can make one realize how these routine activities are fun.

2.Practice Right when You Wake up.

Practicing mindfulness early in the morning can be of much importance. This is because it sets one's nervous system for the rest of the day, and thus increases the chances of other mindful moments within the day.

If one finds it hard to practice mindfulness just after waking up, one should try it after having their breakfast.

3.Let Your Mind Wander.

Being 'busy' mentally is usually an asset to any human. This is because a human brain and mind are designed in such a way that they keep on roaming around. These beneficial brain changes are usually attributed to the act of noticing that your mind has wandered, and then non-judgmentally bringing it back. This act of noticing is usually the act of mindfulness.

4.Keep it Short.

Mindfulness is an act that should be practiced several times a day rather than just setting aside a lengthy session in a day. This is because the human brain responds better to bursts of mindfulness rather than a single lengthy session.

For example, occasionally in a day, one can tune their body to focus on maybe how their clothes feel on their body in that moment, or even how they breathe at that moment.

5.Practice Mindfulness while You Wait.

Waiting is one of the common things that makes most people frustrated. Being kept at the reception of an office for almost an hour or even being stuck in traffic in not an experience anybody likes to have. Waiting, however, can be of much importance when one sees it as an opportunity to practice mindfulness.

For example, while stuck in traffic, one can focus on maybe how the movement of the cars is happening or even focus on how the shoes feel on their feet.

6.Pick a Prompt to Remind You to be Mindful.

It is usually human nature to forget. It is only normal, therefore, for one to rely on something that reminds them of something. In this case one can choose any routine activity that will help you to be mindful. This activity can be maybe drinking coffee.

7.Learn to Meditate.

Meditation is usually taken to be like the language to mindfulness. Normally, one has first to learn the language before they can speak the language. It is in the same manner that one has first to learn how to meditate in order to cultivate one's mindfulness skills. Meditation helps one tap into mindfulness with ease.

In conclusion, mindfulness is not a luxury in life. It is an art that helps one improve their brain's focus, and thus reduce their stress in life. This in the end leads to a better self.

Killing Procrastination

Are you fond of avoiding or putting off tasks? Does this action dispute with your true values and beliefs? It is high time you step back and ask yourself authentic questions. How responsible are you to accomplish the tasks in the course of time (or not)? If it is not practical to abide with it then ask yourself what else you can pull off to transform your life's situations in order to avoid executing the same task later.

Do you still find yourself procrastinating certain work that is harmonious with your real values and is essential to achieve your goals? These are the task that requires your energy and positive attitude of learning how to finish it more efficiently and within the deadline. Here is a guide on how you can accomplish your task in your best interest without procrastinating.

1.Stop Worrying

If you take a pause you will notice that we spend most of our time worrying about what is required of us to do instead of focusing our time on actually performing the task that needs to be done. Considerably, it is possible that if we redirected time wasted on worrying and thinking about the task and invest it in more useful manner, you will realize you are almost finishing your task(s).

Usually, this is easier said than done. Firstly, start this process by use of consciousness to acknowledge the times in any given moment when you discover yourself full of worry and rumination. When you discover this, use this incident as a chance to remind yourself to convert your energy in a proper creative manner.

2.Start Small

Once you start working on your task you actually realize it is less demanding than they appear to be. When you are faced with huge workloads or obstacles you can decide to break down tasks into smaller categories and assigning a deadline for each task group. This is an effective and efficient way to carry out your tasks in order to accomplish them on time.

If your desk is stuck with a pile of papers and reports, it is easy to glimpse at it and become overpowered by its absolute weight. Preferably, look at the pile of papers for literally what it is (one simple sheet of paper on top of another sheet). By doing this you will be able to take things to step by step, and at the end you realize you have accomplished a great deal within a short time.

3.Save the Cost of Wasting Time

Do you know the more time you waste on avoiding something uninteresting, troublesome, and repulsive, the more it will cost you later to perform the same task? No matter how much you evade a task it rarely vanishes on its own. It will calmly wait for you to work on it, and during the procrastination period, it is possible that it has piled up into some vulgar appendage for you pull off.

Let's take this example: take out a clean sheet of paper and subdivide it into two columns. Under the first column write down a list of all the irresistible reasons to perform the task (rewards and benefits). Under the second column make a list of all possible reasons to not to do the work (they are the benefits you believe to achieve by avoiding the task). Have a look at the two columns. Which do you see is longer and more reasonable? It is likely that the most effective choice is to take care of the task now rather than later.

4.Challenge Negative Beliefs

It is a common thing for cognitive distortions to get in the way and obstruct the completion of unsatisfactory tasks within the deadline. Start by discovering and observing your own thoughts with better care and clarity. Do you notice what messages you might be sending yourself via a habitual loop of thinking?

Using CBT, begin to rethink your thoughts and identify negative thoughts. Consider them merely for what they are (just thoughts). Thoughts are just created words and pictures that run through your mind. They will bear meaning if you assign them one. Challenge your ridiculous and negative values and question the soundness of your thoughts with absolute apprehensive knowledge. The moment you start thinking positively you reap more benefits.

5.Search for Hidden Rewards

Identify the expected rewards and benefits you will achieve upon accomplishing (and not finishing) the undesirable task that you may have left without notice. What is the short-term and permanently secondary gains that you can anticipate after completing or not completing the task? For instance, a few people procrastinate due to subliminal fear of failure, or because they are such perfectionists. On the other hand, consider how deciding to finish the task will adversely result in reducing anxiety and stress.

CHAPTER 5 - STEP BY STEP GUIDE TO SELF-HELP CBT

Now that you understand what to expect from CBT, the next important thing to understand is how to handle the situation on your own when it arises. The step-by-step guide is very easy to follow, as long as you really believe in yourself and understand that it takes a bit of practice to do it properly and with true change for your future.

Step 1: Identify the base of your troubles

We all have different things that make life difficult for us. In order to make your life more bearable, you need to correctly identify the base of your problems and to use the CBT method to fix it over time. For example, for some people the issue will be anxiety, for others, depressions, for some addiction, and for others still it could be a traumatic event from the past. This is an important step because by understanding what it is that makes you worries the most, it will be easier for you to recognize the negative thoughts that are associated with these things that affect your mental health.

Step 2: Begin the completion of goals

The next step is to start the completion of tasks that will help you achieve the small goals that you have set for you near future. The reason why you must begin this process is because you are preparing for the next stage of CBT, which is the understanding of the thoughts that are about to appear and stop you from achieving your goals.

Step 3: Consider the thoughts and try to avert them to new ones

Almost as soon as you begin to work on a task, the negative thoughts that always stop you from achieving your goals will appear. But do not follow those thoughts. Instead, hold on to them, take a moment to analyze where they are coming from and why they are trying to ruin your time, and then try to avert them to different thoughts. For example, instead of worrying about failing at the completion of a task, avert the thought to that of a great experience. Think of how wonderful it is to have the opportunity to dream of a better life and to have the courage to go for it. Do not focus on the possibility of failing, instead, only focus on all the things that you will learn along the way. This is what it means to avert the thoughts to new ones, and although it is a slow process when you first try to do so, it will eventually become much easier to do, until it eventually become part of your usual thought process. You will notice that once you are aware of the negative thoughts and you have developed the ability to create new thoughts, you will form new, positive habits that will then be once again be applicable to future experiences and they will help you to build a better life for yourself.

Step 4: Make these actions daily habits

The final thing to keep in mind is that you must now learn to use these steps on a daily basis whenever you are faced with a situation where your thoughts are ruining your ability to achieve your goals. This is why it takes time to develop a new way of looking at your life and the world around you. It may even take a few months to complete this process successfully, so do not give up if you are faced with difficulties along the way. Remember that you can use the CBT method of dealing with bad habits even when you are dealing with the CBT process itself!

CHAPTER 6 - HOW CBT HELPS TREAT ADDICTION

Addiction is a chronic disease that impairs the proper functioning of both the body and the brain. The affected person indulges in a substance or behavior whose rewards incentivize their repeated use despite the fact the addictive substance or behavior is detrimental to their health. When you mention addiction, people automatically imagine drugs and alcohol, forgetting that even behaviors such as sex and gambling could be addictive as well. The affected person commonly loses control, continues to indulge regardless of the negative effects, and fails when they attempt to quit. Addiction has a negative impact on pretty much all angles of an individual's life—family, school, work, neighborhood, and social.

Addictive substances lead to the secretion of dopamine and activate the brain reward centers. Addiction affects the brain's proper functioning and the affected individuals tend to ignore the fact their addiction is debilitating them. As time goes, the rewarding effect of the addictive substance or behavior becomes the dominant aspect of the affected person's life.

There are many myths surrounding the problem of addiction. The truth is that there's no simple answer to explain the cause of addiction. Although biological factors might make an individual susceptible to addiction, it is usually a combination of environmental, social, and psychological factors that lead to the development of an addiction.

Addictions start as recreational activities and gather strength as the individual indulges in the drug or vice more frequently. Some drugs and vices have a high risk of addiction whereas others have a significantly low risk of addiction. But every addiction is inclined towards always needing more. For instance, if you are addicted to alcohol, you will continuously need to consume more alcohol than you previously did in order to activate the reward centers in your brain. Eventually, it gets to a point that you cannot function normally without indulging your addictive vice or substance.

Symptoms of Addiction

- Having the need to indulge in the vice or substance regularly: for instance, if you are addicted to alcohol, you might find yourself needing to partake of it several times throughout the day. It doesn't matter what you are doing. You have to stop everything and run to the bar and drown a few bottles to set your mind straight.

- An intense urge for the drug or vice: in this case, you cannot function normally unless you have indulged in your addictive vice. Once the urge comes down on you, you cannot wish it away, and you must cave.
- Needing bigger portions: in the early days of sex addiction, maybe having sex twice a week was enough, then it became thrice a week, then four times, five times, six times, and now you have to perform sex like five times in a single day. As a matter of fact, addictions light up the brain reward centers, and the more you use an addictive substance or vice, the harder it gets to activate these reward centers, causing you to need more of the addictive substance in order to actually feel good.
- Maintaining a supply: since you have conditioned yourself that you cannot live without a particular vice, you want to have a big supply of the addictive vice. For instance, if you are addicted to smoking marijuana, you keep a stash of it in your house and cars, so that you can easily retrieve it.
- Spending money on the vice even though you are financially lacking: most people who do hard drugs tend to live in poor neighborhoods, and they tend to prioritize their addictions over everything else. That's exactly why some people resort to crime to fund their addictive habits.
- Failing in your attempts to stop: you may try to stop indulging in the vice, but you always come up short. The vice has held you as a hostage and it is hard to break from the destructive addiction.
- Not meeting obligations or work responsibilities because of the vice or substance: once your vice makes it hard for you to fulfill your obligations, you obviously have an addiction. For instance, if you are an excessive drinker, you might start falling back on your work commitments, and this could hinder you from being a productive person or reaching your important goals.
- Continuing to indulge in the vice when you know too well that it's affecting your life: if you are an alcoholic, it would probably result in the disintegration of your personal relationships, and yet you couldn't be bothered to change your ways. It indicates that addiction has taken control over your life and you prioritize the things that make you feel good over everything else.
- Doing risky things when you have partaken of your addictive vices or substances: for instance, if you are addicted to alcohol, you will find yourself more often causing public disturbances, over

speeding, and indulging in other obnoxious behaviors without minding the fact that you could get yourself into trouble.

Types of Addiction

The truth is that you can be addicted to almost anything, and this happens when someone continues to indulge in a vice or substance even though there are negative consequences. The following are some common types of addictions:

- Alcohol addiction: it is a legal substance that is consumed around the world, yet if left ungoverned; alcohol could literally ruin your life. An alcohol addiction means that you have to start your day with alcohol and throughout the day you will be looking forward to the end of your shift so that you can run to your locals and drown more beers. Apart from the physical and psychological dependence on alcohol, it could also ruin your finances.
- Drug addiction: what usually starts as recreational use of drugs leads most people into a pit of addiction that ruins relationships, families, and finances in its wake.
- Gambling addiction: when they start out, they are hoping to win the big monies, but eventually they become addicted to the game, and the adrenaline rush associated with winning.
- Eating disorders: people with eating disorders have unhealthy eating habits. The commonest eating disorders are anorexia and bulimia. Anorexia is characterized by severe restriction of calories whereas bulimia is characterized by binge eating then purging yourself of the food through vomiting or excessive physical exercises. Also, eating too much can become an addiction, which usually results in obesity.
- Gaming addiction: there a lot of people nowadays, especially teens, who spend more time in the virtual world than the real world. If not managed well, the gaming world can quickly escalate into an addiction.
- Pornography addiction: a lot of people are guilty of stealing glances at pornography severally throughout their lives. But once watching pornography graduates into an addiction, it creates a serious problem that gradually ruins the affected person's life. Pornography addiction causes a person to keep stretching the limits on what more extreme sexual acts they can find. The sexual partners of people with pornography addiction have a very

difficult time because their partners have some twisted perception of sex.

Causes of Addiction

Addiction is caused by one or a combination of the following factors:

- Low self-esteem: when someone is suffering from low self-esteem, they have a very poor perception of self. This may lead them to indulge in various vices hoping to escape from their reality, and eventually, it leads to an addiction.
- Mental illnesses: addiction could come about as a result of suffering from various other mental illnesses. According to the National Alliance on Mental Illness, 50% of people who suffer from addiction have other serious mental health conditions.
- Peer pressure: this especially true for people who are still at an impressionable age. Most people start drinking alcohol and smoking marijuana in high school, where peer pressure is at the peak, and they are at risk of developing an addiction because they lack insight.
- Trauma: trauma might also lead a person into seeking alternative worlds through drugs and it could lead them into an addiction.

Treating Addiction with CBT

Step 1: understanding the effects of addiction

People who have an addiction might want to stop, but they are so deep in the vice and they are helpless against the urge to partake of it. In most cases, addiction symptoms such as over-dependence on a vice hardly drive a person into seeking restorative measures. However, it is the effects of addiction, mostly broken relationships and ruined finances that cause a person to seek treatment.

Thus, the first order of business for a therapist is to establish the magnitude of loss before the patient came looking for help. These are some of the questions that are asked:

- What diseases have arisen from the addiction?
- Neurological and emotional effects of overindulgence in your vice?
- Legal consequences of your addiction
- Social problems arising from your addiction
- Workplace problems arising from addiction

At this stage, the therapist also assists the patient to come up with their short term and long term goals that promote full recovery. The achievement of goals greatly depends on how motivated an individual is. But it may also depend on the extent of addiction. People who have been addicted for a long time will take longer to see any progress as opposed to people who have been addicted for a short period of time.

The goals may be such as:

- Reduce my dependence on my vice from daily indulgence to once in a week
- Spend quality time with family and friends
- Stop hanging out with people who influence me to partake of my vice
- Maintain a healthy diet
- Start performing physical exercises

Step 2: understanding the recovery process

It is also critical to prepare the individual mentally about the various tools and processes that will help them get their normal life back. At this stage, they get to learn about the skills and tools that will help them overcome their addiction.

- Recognize triggers: no matter what your addiction might be, there had to be something that compelled you to take the initial step in your vice. Your therapist helps you understand various aspects such per pressure and idleness that encouraged you to start indulging in a vice.
- Avoid: there are many CBT exercises to help you dodge situations that encourage you to indulge in various vices.
- Cope: your addiction won't go away without a fight. But then there are enough CBT exercises to fight away the unpleasant emotions and feelings arising from non-indulgence of your vice.

Step 3: understanding the root of your problem

There are various reasons that can lead you down the destructive path of addiction. But besides acknowledging these reasons, you have to understand precisely how they drove you into these addictions. Some of the root causes of addiction include:

- Stress
- Low self-esteem

- Peer pressure
- Trauma
- Mental health issues
- Genetics

Step 4: behavior modification

Perform CBT techniques to help you overcome your addiction.

- Journaling: one of the most powerful techniques is journaling, which involves writing down your thoughts and feelings. Write down about your urges and resist the temptation. If a pattern emerges, see how you can modify your behavior.
- Relaxed breathing: whenever the urges come along, you can start performing breathing exercises, and these urges should go away.

CHAPTER 7 - 7 TECHNIQUES TO IMPROVE YOUR FREEDOM FROM SOCIAL ANXIETY

As you learn about Cognitive Behavioral Therapy you are probably curious about the techniques that are actually used in it. In this section, you will learn about the various different techniques that are used during Cognitive Behavioral Therapy. The methods may vary during the therapy but the intended end result is usually the same. It is the prerogative of the therapist to recommend or use the most suitable techniques according to their assessment of the client.

The following are some of the techniques that therapists use during Cognitive Behavioral Therapy:

1. Thought Recording

In this technique the person will be asked to maintain a record of their thoughts over time. They have to note their thoughts down in some sort of book and maintain the record. Thought recording is especially important when the person had a habit of thinking negatively. Writing the thought down gives them a chance to look at it and evaluate it. They examine the thought in a logical manner and when they realize that it is pointless or baseless, they can disregard it from there. This habit of noting thoughts down will help the person be more objective in their assessment rather than subjective. This technique helps the person determine the validity or invalidity of the thoughts they have. It also allows them to notice any pattern of negative thinking so they can tackle the problem at hand.

2. Technique Based on Imagery

In this technique, the person has to recall a particular situation in their mind where they may have reacted badly or any negative emotions may have emerged. Recreating this in their mind is easy because the brain tends to remember bad experiences for quite some time. Recollecting the scene will allow the person to remember how they felt and the way they behaved and also consider why they did so. In this recreation, they will get a chance to be more objective and assess how they could have reacted better or thought about things in a more positive way. This technique allows the person to improve their thighs or reactions when faced with a similar situation in the future.

3. Technique Based on Pie Charts

When a person is faced with an anxiety inducing situation, they will tend to have an automatic thought as soon as this anxiety arises in them. This will usually occur due to a particular factor. This negative automatic thought should be noted down. The person should write down the various reasons that could be responsible for the anxiety inducing situation to have occurred. Along with the automatic thought, each of these reasons should be assigned a particular number to denote the possibility of it. Then place these in a pie chart and evaluate if your automatic thought was really sensible or if the pie chart makes more sense.

4. Exposure Hierarchies

Anxiety may occur in different ways and at different levels. Certain situations will only make you a little anxious while another different situation can heighten the sense of anxiety. There is thus a hierarchy of levels that a person should note down in order of anxiety inducing situations from highest to lowest levels. The therapist will then help the client tackle each of these situations one by one so that they feel less anxious the next time they face it. It may be hard to completely overcome the anxiety of the highest levels but you will be better equipped to deal with them in the future. As each anxiety-inducing factor is dealt with, they should only move on to the next one when the anxiety reduces at least by half for the previous factor.

5. Behavioral Experiments

The experiments involved in this technique are designed in a way that they will make the person test the rationale behind each decision they make or thought they have. You might have two different thoughts on how a certain action may pan out. The therapist may recommend that you try it out and find out what really happens. If you are conflicted about what to do in the first place, they will tell you to try both and see the outcomes. Then assess the outcomes and see which action worked in your favor. This will help you determine the course of action that you should take in the future. You will also realize which types of thoughts are more constructive for you and what brings you down. This will motivate you to think and act in a better way.

6. SMART Goals

With an idea of what to avoid, you now can move on to understanding what makes a goal good. When you are trying to learn new things, acronyms are always helpful, as they give you one thing to remember to use as a prompt for all of the parts. When thinking about goals, remember that you want to set SMART goals in order to maximize efficiency and effectiveness. SMART stands for specific, measurable, attainable, relevant, and timely. By remembering this acronym, you have the prompt necessary to create goals that are effective and achievable.

7. Scheduling Pleasant Activities

This technique or activity is actually as simple as it sounds. Here the person will be asked to create a schedule of doing things they really enjoy. However, they should make sure that none of it has a negative effect on anyone else around them. This activity is usually recommended to people who suffer from stress or depression. It helps them feel better and reduces cortisol levels. The activity does not have to be something very complicated, expensive or even time consuming. Just dedicating a few minutes to doing something you really like can be very beneficial. When a person carries this out and sees the positive emotions it brings out, they will be more inclined to do this in the future. The therapist may recommend that the person schedule this activity for themselves at least once a week. No matter how busy you are or how hectic your work life is, you can definitely do this. You can also do some simple pleasant activities on a daily basis to make yourself happier. It can be as easy as making a nice cup of tea and reading a few pages of your favorite book in the morning or before sleeping.

There are many other techniques that therapists use during Cognitive Behavioral Therapy. You can learn such techniques even through online courses or through a self-help book. Cognitive Behavioral Therapy techniques are meant to help the person change their negative thoughts pattern into a more positive one and the same goes for their behavioral patterns. It is crucial that the person goes through with these activities and practices them from time to time even after the therapy sessions are completed. You can find out about many more techniques through other resources on Cognitive Behavioral Therapy.

CHAPTER 8 - USE THE RIGHT KIND OF EXERCISE

We all know that exercise is very beneficial for the human species. A ton of studies and experts have pointed that out to us. However, some "experts" have been preaching some unhealthy principles of exercise, which has unfortunately caused billions of people to look at exercise in a way that doesn't necessarily benefit their bodies, health, and certainly not stress levels.

Recommending certain types of exercises can be very controversial because there are many different opinions out there, and many of them are based on pseudoscience, or studies that don't even exist. In this book, we will use a science-based approach that allows you to do enjoyable and relaxing exercises, which will both benefit your stress levels and optimize your health.

Exercise and chronic stress have a weird relationship. On one hand, we all know that regular exercise has a large amount of health benefits. However, on the other hand, you will know that exercising too much can also cause chronic stress.

Too much or too little?

I believe there are just as many people in the Western world who exercise too much as there are people who exercise too little. Furthermore, exercising too much is just as bad for your health, if not worse, than exercising too little. When you exercise too much, your body raises cortisol. This is called overtraining and is a form of chronic stress. As you know, when cortisol rises, your stress response is on, which will naturally make you feel stressed and tired.

Overtraining has many of the same side effects as chronic stress because the physical reaction is pretty much the same. Overtraining will leave you extremely fatigued and oftentimes even depressed. Exercising too much is one of the last things you want to do if you suffer with chronic stress. However, not exercising at all is also very unhealthy, so you should not avoid exercise entirely either.

Instead, you want to find that "sweet spot" where you get the amazing health benefits of regular exercise while you avoid exercising too much and the unwanted side effects that come with that. The keys to find this sweet spot are to listen to your body and create a balanced exercise program that leaves you feeling energized, not tired, after performing it.

If you have a wearable device that can measure your heart rate and/or heart rate variability, these can also be great to use to check if you have been exercising too much and if you have recovered properly, so that you're ready to exercise more. If your heart rate drops quickly during the night and if your HRV is high during the night, these are signs that you are recovering well. If your heart rate lowers late and your HRV is low during the night, you should probably not go for a physically challenging exercise program the next day. Instead, you should simply relax and recover. However, in this book we are going to assume that you just listen to your body. That's the free solution and it often works just fine for our purpose of relieving stress.

So, how can you listen to your body? It's pretty simple. There are two rules that you should follow if you want your exercise routine to lower stress rather than raise it. The first rule is: **If you feel too fatigued to exercise, don't do it**. Spending hours on a treadmill will just make you more fatigued. If you do want to get some exercise in that situation it should be low-level physical activity, which doesn't put too much stress on your body.

The second rule is: If you feel like you have less energy after exercising than you had before, you have been exercising too hard or too much**. When lower stress is your goal, exercising should always give you more energy, not less.**

These are the two exercise rules to keep in mind when you exercise to lower stress levels. When you are chronically stressed, you don't want to do anything that puts more stress on your body, which is exactly what exercising too hard or for too long does. Instead, you want to do something that is enjoyable and makes you feel good afterwards. Now that you know what the main principles of your stress-relieving exercise routine should be, let's take a look at which types of exercise you can use to get the best benefits for your stress levels and your health.

Low-level Physical Exercise

low-level physical activity can offer some great benefits, and I recommend that you use this type of exercise as much as you like, as long as your body is okay with it. These types of exercises are least likely to worsen stress. Rather, they should feel very relaxing.

Low-level physical exercise can be a walk, a yoga session, an easy bike ride, a hike or anything else that isn't very physically challenging. Doing low-level physical exercise every day can be very good for your stress levels, and it doesn't have to be that difficult. All you have to do is walk around for a bit (preferably in nature).

Resistance Training

If you have the energy for it, doing some resistance training once in a while can be very good for your resilience to stress and your overall health.

Resistance training is when your body pushes against a force. The most common types of resistance training are weight lifting and other types of strength training. It sounds stressful for the body to do some heavy weight lifting, you might think. And you would be completely right. However, it is a bit more complex than that.

Resistance training does put some stress on your body in the short term. This is not necessarily a bad thing if you have a proper routine, though. The key to a proper resistance training routine is enough recovery time. I recommend six to nine days. When you do resistance training this way, you will make your body momentarily stressed after the exercise. However, when you allow your body to recover for six to nine days, it will increase your resilience to stress in the long term. So, when you follow this routine, you exchange some short-term stress for long-term stress relief and resistance.

However, if you're already very stressed, you might not want the momentary stress increase from resistance training. That's why I recommend that you only do resistance training if you feel like you have enough energy to do it. If you do, it can be very beneficial for you and make you more resilient to stress over time.

Aerobic Exercise

Aerobic exercise is very popular and it can be beneficial. However, it can also require a lot of effort and time, which can be quite stressful.

Aerobic exercise, also known as endurance training or cardio, can be something like running, swimming or cycling. Or it can be almost any sports that require constant movement. If you have an existing practice of this type of exercise that you like, you can keep doing that. Especially if it also includes good social relationships. However, aerobic exercise is typically not the first type of exercise that I would recommend for people with chronic stress issues. That's because endurance training is oftentimes seen as something you must do every day, or at least three to four times a week, for 30-60 minutes to get good results. This can be a lot of time for you to invest, which you really don't have to. Plus, it can be very taxing for your body and just put more stress on it. Also, you really don't have to do aerobic exercise for several hours every week to see good benefits from your exercise routine.

Like I said, if you have an aerobic exercise that you like that makes you feel better, you can keep doing that. However, I would only do aerobic exercise several times a week for the fun it could provide, not necessarily for the benefits. If you have fun doing it, it can be great. However, if you just want the health benefits and better resilience to stress in as short time as possible, there are better ways.

HIIT

High-intensity interval training (HIIT) gives you a combination of the good effects of aerobic exercise and resistance training in a very short amount of time. It improves your mitochondria, it helps with detoxification and weight loss[83], and dramatically increases growth hormone levels. In other words, it is perhaps the best way to exercise for your health.

In a HIIT workout you shift between doing high-intensity intervals and resting. For example, you can sprint for 60 seconds, and then sit or lie down for 90 seconds. And when I say sprint, I really mean sprint. You want to get some real effort into those 60 seconds, so your heart rate rises as much as possible. Because when your heart rate is high, you will get the benefits of aerobic exercise while you're relaxing between the intervals.

However, HIIT doesn't have to be running. It can be anything that allows you to do a high-intensity interval and get your heart rate up quickly. The best thing about HIIT is that it takes very little time. You simply do the intervals for as long as you can, or for a maximum of 15 minutes in total. This means that you will, at most, be doing six sprints or other high-intense intervals. Furthermore, you only have to do this once a week. Just once a week will give you amazing benefits. You don't have to put more time into it. When you combine HIIT with low-level physical activity throughout the week, your exercise routine will require almost no time and it will give a whole bunch of benefits. Your resilience to stress should also increase significantly.

Again, it's important to mention that you should always listen to your body. If your fatigue becomes worse after doing HIIT, it might not be the right thing for you at that moment. If that is the case, you can try to do HIIT later when you are less stressed. However, as with resistance training, HIIT should only put stress on your body in the short term whereas it should increase your resilience to stress in the long term.

Generally, HIIT is very beneficial, and it probably won't hurt you to try it once. You can just do one high-intensity interval for 60 seconds and see how you feel the next day or a few days after. If you feel better, you can go for more the following week. If you feel worse, you might want to wait some extra time before you try it again. Recover

When it comes to exercising, the most important thing you can do to minimize stress is to ensure that your body is fully recovered after a workout before you start a new one. If you feel like your body isn't fully recovered after exercising, you should relax or only do some light movement until you're fully recovered.

I have mentioned this a few times already, but I really wanted to finish this exercise chapter with this recommendation, which is the most important thing you should include into your exercise routine. When your body recovers well, you are less stressed. The opposite happens if you don't allow your body to get the recovery that it needs.

CHAPTER 9 - YOU ARE YOUR OWN CURE

Living with anxiety means that you are always on edge. You're living a life that is propelled by fear. This makes it difficult to find any type of enjoyment to speak of. Your mind is always stuck on the "what ifs" that may happen. Rather than being able to live in the moment, all your thoughts are directed either on the guilt of the past or the unpredictable prospects of the future.

This is no way to live, and the fact that you're reading this book shows that you don't want to continue to live that way. An anxiety disorder is a common occurrence in today's modern world. Things move fast and the ability to take your time and relish at the moment is fleeting at best. However, it is comforting to know that you don't have to live that way. You can do something about it.

Google anxiety and you will be immediately inundated with options of all kinds. Some will promise to heal you through herbs and diets, others offer you a wide array of medications, and then some will tell you to just slough it off, and things will get better. You and I both know and understand that your choices for reclaiming your life are many.

While there has been a great deal of success in many of these methods, we encourage you to attempt to resolve your anxiety issues in a more natural way. Your brain and your body have already been designed to heal itself. It's just that, most of us have lost touch with how to communicate with our bodies effectively. We go through life like an automaton, jumping from one function to another, void of feelings and confidence. However, if we learn to tap into our own natural resources, health and recovery are often just a short distance away.

The reality is that we have the power to heal ourselves within us. In most cases, you won't need expensive medications, pay hundreds of dollars to therapists, or buy into a lot of expensive gadgetry. There are steps you can take right now, techniques you can apply the moment you feel your anxiety start to rise to help your mind to reach a calmer state so you can add more positive feelings to your life.

Getting in the Right Frame of Mind

Regardless of the method, you choose to aid you to recovery, keep these basic points in mind before you begin any treatment. We live in a world full of negativity, so it's no wonder that we drift off into the negativity land without effort. The challenge, though, is to redirect our thoughts to the more positive. This will be the first step in getting our thinking back on track.

Show Gratitude: Cultivate a spirit of gratitude. Believe it or not, this is a mental exercise that all of us can practice. This is not just to be thankful for the basic things in life but to think deeper in that same line of thought. Making a concerted effort to at least feel gratitude inside can start us thinking more positively.

Our world is rushed, and often, we don't take the time to appreciate the things we receive without asking. Good health, a family that cares, a regular paycheck, or just being able to have a meal on the table. In the beginning, you may have to set up reminders to stop and show your appreciation for what you have.

We are all accustomed to using cues to remind us of other activities, so it just makes sense that we would use similar cues to remind us to think on more positive lines. You do this enough, and eventually, your mind will start to do it automatically, without thought or planning. Sometimes, we do this without noticing. For example, if you know you're going in to work with a very demanding boss, you mentally prepare yourself. You walk in with a spirit of wariness, and you've thought of everything you can think of to help you get through the day smoothly. You do the same if you plan to visit a sick friend. The same should also be true when you are preparing for a potential anxiety attack. The more you prepare your mind ahead of time, the easier it will be when you are actually working to push that anxiety back down to a level where it belongs.

Reject Your Inner Sensations: Next, you want to recognize those negative thoughts and refuse to accept them. A gift is not a gift until you accept it. So, if your mind is flooded with negativity, realize that you have the option to say no to it. You are not compelled to accept any thought or feeling just because it came from your subconscious mind.

Our subconscious mind has been trained by our myriad of experiences that we go through from the moment of birth. Sadly, we have often forgotten the experiences that led to our negative thinking and only the thoughts remain. Just as we said earlier on this book, change is a natural part of life, and any experience you had that shaped your negativity and fears most likely no longer exists. Learning to say no to such things will help you stabilize your mind and put you in a more positive perspective.

Find Your Safety Zone: No matter how bad we think something may be or has the potential to be, it is always easier to handle when we know that we have a safe place to run to. Our safety zone doesn't always have to be a physical place to hide. It can be a form of meditation or just a mental state you train your mind to run to when things get to be too much.

Because of the crazy world we live in, most of us have forgotten how to live. We are constantly on the watch, focusing our attention on potential dangers, threats, malice, and pain. When we fall into that line of thinking, we feel everything are not safe. Start making it a habit to look for the good things in your life. They are there, hidden away behind a wealth of badness, but you can find them. You just have to look for them.

Change Your Inner Critic: We all have that inner voice that is constantly reminding us of our past failures and our faults. This is not a characteristic exclusive to those with an anxiety disorder. It is common to all of us. But we have to start making a concerted effort to put that voice on mute. Those harsh words were drilled into us years ago, possibly when we were children and couldn't do everything right. But now, we have to change that dynamic. Up until this point, it has been a one-way conversation with that tiny voice buzzing all these negatives in your ear. It's time for you to start talking back to it.

Our inner critic acts like a judge that has nothing good to say. It judges the quality of our work, predicts how other people will view you, and makes you feel guilty and ashamed at every turn. It mocks you, teases you, and bullies you. He doesn't care about your feelings and has only one goal, and that is to prevent you from having any joy in life by questioning and doubting everything you do.

Identify the Judge: One of the first things you need to do is to identify your judge. If his voice is constantly ringing in your ear, chances are that you are not even noticing it anymore, you are automatically responding to it without even being aware of its negative prodding. You'll notice when your judge is there when you finally get up enough nerve to tackle something and suddenly your energy starts to wane, you begin to question yourself, or without reason, you lose interest. Recognize, at this point, that it is your judge, your inner critic who is taunting you.

Stop and listen to what he has to say but don't respond to it. Don't resist his words because that will only build up the anxiety in you. Start a dialogue with him, refuting all of his arguments. For example:

Critic: "Why are you doing that? People will think you're strange."

You: "So what if you say that. It doesn't mean it's true."

Critic: "Do you really think that others will care about what you do?"

You: "Who cares what other people think. Do you think I want to live with others judging me?"

Critic: "You're not going to be able to finish that so why even bother."

You: "I'm doing this for me, not for someone else."

Whatever you hear your inner critic tell you, don't remain silent. It's a tiny little voice in all of us. But the important thing is to acknowledge what he says, respond to it, and then keep moving on. That little voice inside our heads is there to serve as a warning to keep us from getting into danger. But there are times when he gets a little too much power and warns us even when there is no threat.

The inner critic rarely goes away. As long as we're living, he will continue to find ways to sabotage our efforts. However, if we can identify who he is, acknowledge that we've heard him and forge on in spite of the fears he creates, his voice will not have as much power over us, and we won't have to worry about succumbing to our fears.

A Word at the Right Time

Another mystical tradition that has done wonders to help relieve anxiety is the use of affirmations. Because you're caught in a loop of negative thinking that has undoubtedly taken its toll. The use of positive affirmations is a great way to verbally interrupt those negative thoughts with something positive. It aids your mind to shift its thinking and gradually guides the mental process in another direction.

You can use these affirmations in three different ways.

•You can say them silently to yourself.

•You can write them down.

•You can say them out loud to yourself.

Anytime you feel overwhelmed with negative thoughts, you can use these positive affirmations to redirect your thoughts in a more positive direction. Some therapists recommend that you make it a habit by attaching your affirmations to something you do every day. For example, every time you get in your car, you repeat your affirmations. Or you could say them every time you go to prepare a meal, put your children to bed, or hang up the phone. The trick here is to make it a regular habit to use these affirmations until they become a natural habit to you.

Some examples of positive affirmations you could make to fight off anxiety:

•I am calm.

•I am a good person.

•I value who I have become.

•I am healthy.

•I feel relaxed.

•I can let go of this stress.

•I am a good student.

•I can make a new friend today.

•I have a good relationship with my family and friends.

There are some basic rules about creating your own affirmations. First, all affirmations must be used in the present tense. Do not make mantras about the future or refer to something in the past. Second, they must always be about you. You are battling your own inner thinking process; therefore, your affirmation should be there to redirect your thinking. This is the only thing you have any control over. And third, they have to be 100% positive. Do not use any words like can't, don't, won't, etc. Instead of saying I can't get angry anymore, rephrase it to say "I am going to stay calm today."

Many people question the value of something as simple as positive affirmations. However, while they are not an actual cure for an anxiety disorder, they are a powerful coping technique that will work for you until you can get the benefit of more long-term treatment options. You can think of them as a means to counteract those negative thoughts while you are working on something else. They are there to give your brain an alternative way of thinking.

While they are commonly used when negative feelings and thoughts pop up, some have found they do better if they start their day with affirmations, letting them start on a more positive note. However, you choose to use them, they can help ease your anxiety in many ways:

•They are a positive distraction and can keep your thoughts from running wild.

•They give you a positive belief. In time, the brain will adapt to the positive phrases and start to adapt to the belief that you are trying to form.

•And they serve as a constant reminder to insert more positive things in your life.

Make sure that the affirmations you choose have personal meaning to you. While you can find a long list of suggestions online, one that you create yourself will have more influence over your thinking than something written by a total stranger.

You need to be committed to using them regularly. It may take time before you begin to see the benefits but if you continue, eventually you'll start to feel the anxious discomfort fade away replaced by something more positive and actually makes you feel good.

CHAPTER 10 - BE RESPONSIBLE FOR YOUR HAPPINESS

So far we have talked about many skills for handling intense emotions, from cognitive skills about changing your thoughts to more behavior oriented ones. We have talked about mindfulness and emotional regulation. However, the most important skill is radical acceptance. This is the idea that even in the most painful situation we have to accept it. This is what makes it radical.

Acceptance does not mean approval. Acceptance means acknowledging the situation you are in as real and there is nothing you can do about it. Many of us spend a lot of time refusing to accept the reality of a situation. We think this isn't fair or wonder why this is happening. These things increase our suffering. Pain is unavoidable in life, but suffering isn't. Pain is what happens when something bad happens; suffering is what happens when we fight against it and refuse to accept it.

Acceptance is non-judgmental. Accepting something doesn't mean you are saying it is good or bad. It means you are acknowledging reality as it is. Imagine that you are driving to work and are stuck in traffic. This is unpleasant in many ways. You might get in trouble for being late to work. But if you think, "This is unfair" and "I can't believe this is happening," you are just going to increase how upset you are. Honking and tailgating the car in front of you won't get you to work any faster. It increases unhappy you are. Imagine the difference between being upset and worked up the entire slow commute to work and accepting the fact you will be late and being at peace in the car.

Accepting reality is the necessary shift that helps genuine and permanent change. You cannot change anything unless you have first accepted it. If you are constantly fighting reality, you'll spend all your time and energy pretending the problem doesn't exist as opposed to fixing the problem. Acceptance isn't about forgiveness or about letting anybody off the hook. The only goal is to put your mind at ease and make yourself happier. You accept reality for yourself.

This is a difficult skill but perhaps the most important one in the book. The more painful and difficult a situation is, the more difficult it will be to accept, and it will usually take longer. This is not a skill that can be mastered in one day even at the best of times. To return to our driving example, if the conclusion of being late will inevitably mean you get fired, it will be much harder to accept that if it is simply talking to your boss. Sometimes you can get to the point of acceptance on something, and then an additional event will trigger you to start fighting reality again. Imagine Karen, a woman whose husband had an affair many years ago. She might have accepted it and moved on with their marriage, allowing things to improve tremendously. But then a young woman, who looks like the woman Karen's husband had an affair with, moves next door, and Karen feels angry and upset once again. She might have to go back to accept reality and not fight it.

As you are working on accepting reality, it might get frustrating. Even if you can accept the painful fact for only thirty seconds, that is thirty seconds of less suffering. Gradually those thirty seconds will grow and grow until you can sustain it.

Most of us have had painful situations in our life that we have naturally come to accept. Perhaps a loved one died, or you did not receive a job you were hoping for. It hurts, but eventually, it is possible to come to terms and accept the new reality. There is a difference between fighting a situation and coming to terms with it. Most of the time, you feel lighter and more at ease once you've accepted a situation. The situation has less power over you, and the pain diminishes. When you think about it, there is less emotional pain.

How do you practice accepting reality?

The first and most important part is that you choose to accept it. You have to buy into the idea that accepting reality will be helpful and make you feel better. If you don't buy in, there's nothing to be done. Part of this involves facing what is happening. Before you can accept something, you have to develop the self-awareness to face it.

Second, if you decide to work on acceptance, the next step is to commit yourself to accept the reality you are fighting. You need to make yourself a promise that starting now, you will accept the situation. The promise is not going to solve itself. Typically even after you have committed, you will find yourself going back to fighting reality, making judgments, thinking about how unfair the situation is, and so on.

Third, you must learn to notice when you start fighting reality again. Notice when you start thinking the situation is not fair or wishing life was otherwise.

Fourth, turn your mind back to acceptance. Every time you notice yourself fighting reality and insisting reality isn't fair, remind yourself you made a promise to accept reality. Remind yourself of your commitment and turn your mind back toward acceptance. You will need to do this over and over again to get the hang of it.

One thing to acknowledge is that everything has a cause. Even this thing that is causing you pain had to have happened because the way the world went. If you think about it, a tsunami is a tragedy that hurts a lot of people, but the reason why it happened is the law of physics. It had to happen that way because it was caused in a particular way. There is no way for it to have been otherwise, given the way the world was.

It is sometimes useful to think of the whole universe as a series of causes. One thing causes other things, moving around like balls on a pool table. Any individual thing had to happen the way it did, given all the other factors and all the things that caused it. There is inevitability in the past and the future. There was no other way it could have gone.

People tend to have some difficulties with this skill. One thing people think is that accepting reality means giving up. But that is not the case. Acceptance means giving up fighting the reality of the situation; it does not preclude you trying to solve the problem. It means you no longer waste time and energy thinking that a situation isn't fair or undeserved. You instead focus on what is necessary to fix the situation.

Second, sometimes people confuse acceptance of the moment for accepting things that haven't happened yet. When they accept the end of a relationship, they think what they need to accept is a lifetime of loneliness. The thing to remember is accepting reality, not things that haven't happened yet. You need to learn to accept that your previous relationship has ended, but there is no reason to accept there won't be a relationship in the future. We cannot possibly know what the future will hold. It is hard enough accepting the present and the past. There is no reason to make things more difficult by accepting the future.

When you are struggling with being alone, what you need to accept is not having a partner at the present moment. There is no need to accept that you will be alone for the rest of your life. The goal is to keep your mind in the present and to practice mindfulness. Radical acceptance cannot help with concerns that are future-oriented.

Another thing people might think is that acceptance means they need to accept negative judgments about themselves. Someone might think, "How can I accept that I am a bad person?" Just as we cannot accept the future, we also cannot accept judgments. Judgments aren't facts; they are perceptions of reality. You have to accept the facts of your life, but the judgments are extraneous. For instance, if you think you are a bad person because you were addicted to drugs and lashed out to people who cared about you, you need to accept those realities. The reality of addiction and the reality of how you treated others are what you need to accept. Bundling that into a judgment of being a bad person is not what you need to accept and is probably not helpful.

A large problem with acceptance is the idea that the situation is too awful and painful to accept. It is easy to feel that something is so horrible that it is impossible to accept. If you've experienced abuse, you could feel that it is too awful to accept. One issue that happens here is the confusion of acceptance with forgiveness. You are practicing acceptance for yourself, not anyone else. You accept it because it will make your life easier, not because it forgives the person who hurts you. Acceptance doesn't work if you do it for other people, and it isn't about other people.

Sometimes people think we need to stay angry to protect ourselves. You might worry that accepting the situation will make you vulnerable. You feel like you are mad, withdrawn, and resentful as a way of protecting yourself from hurt. The problem is the way that you are trying to protect yourself is causing you suffering in the present. You aren't preventing yourself from being hurt by being angry, but you are causing yourself emotional pain.

Additionally, remember that acceptance doesn't mean approval. The reality, in a sense, doesn't care about whether or not we approve of it. It exists regardless of how we feel. Acceptance is about acknowledging what reality is.

When you start to accept things, you can then begin to think about how you can make the best of things. This means many different things in different contexts. Sometimes it means you should learn what you can from the situation and develop increased empathy from experience. Sometimes you can think about ways you can make the situation better. It is important to think in the long term. Getting drunk may make you feel better in the moment, but it will not feel good in the morning. Meditate, read a good book, or take a walk through nature.

One thing that may help is the realization that life isn't supposed to be easy. Life is supposed to be hard. Hard things happen to everybody. Hard things are part of what develops character and makes you the person who you are. When we think that life is unfair for having difficult things happening, we aren't acknowledging the reality that life is complicated.

There is always something you can learn from difficulty. You can always grow. Even if you feel wounded and damaged by whatever happened, it is possible for you to move forward. Life never ends until it is over. Until that moment, there is always the possibility to get stronger and better as a human being. Accepting the reality of life is part of that.

CHAPTER 11 - HAVE SELF-DISCIPLINE

At this very moment, you have a big decision to make. You have the choice of staying in your comfort zone, with all your old patterns and habits, living in a way that feels as though you're always missing out. Or you can decide right now that you will use this book as the motivation you've been needing to become your greatest self. This could really be the turning point where you start to develop self-discipline and amazing willpower. This is your choice, and only you can make it. So, what do you need to do in order to improve your willpower and self-discipline?

When it comes to achieving the goals and happiness that you want out of life, there is one simple thing you can do that will increase your chances of success 10 fold: improve your self-discipline. While the requirements to achieve your goals will vary based on the specifics, they will all have one thing in common, dedication and hard work will get you there, and self-discipline will make it possible.

Studies show that the more self-discipline and self-control a person has, the happier that person is as they tend to feel as though they are generally more prepared for anything that life can throw at them. This is because, while those without self-discipline spend time motivating themselves to do things, those with self-discipline simply did them which makes them more productive overall.

While those who lack self-discipline likely think that it is an innate behavior, in all actuality it is a skill which means that like any skill it can be improved with practice over time. There are a number of ways that you can strengthen your resolve and improve your ability to maintain your self-discipline even when it may seem difficult or impossible to do so; first, however, you must understand that it is up to you, and no one else, to make better choices in the first place. Your future self is directly influenced by what you choose to do in the present, do yourself a favor and choose wisely.

The human mind is designed to enjoy cause and effect, and indeed, often goes too far and finds patterns where there are none. When it comes to improving your self-discipline, you can use this too your advantage as after the first few instances of persevering and achieving your goals, thus releasing serotonin, the chemical which causes pleasure, your mind will link self-discipline with achieving goals and be anxious to do so more often in an effort to repeat the process. As such, while it will be difficult to power through and ignore all possible distractions at first, it will be easier than that the second time, even easier the third time and will eventually feel like the easiest thing in the world.

This idea exemplifies the paradox principle which states that it is better to do the difficult thing in the present as that will make it easier to do in the future. Inversely this means that if you had started something the first time you thought about it you would be an expert at it by now.

Another way to ensure that you will fully commit to something even if you have not yet mastered the art of self-discipline is to apply the buy-in principle. The buy-in principle states that the greater the personal stake in a project, the harder you will try to ensure that the project doesn't fail. When attempting to break into new fields it is best to take on a single new project at a time as over committing to several projects, even if you have the self-discipline to finish what you start, will only lead to several subpar projects and no outstanding ones.

This is an example of the magnification principle which states that if you dilute your focus you dilute your results. In this ever-connected world, it can be extremely difficult to take the time to focus on a single task at a time. What separates the truly successful from the pretenders is their ability to focus all of their concentration on the right task at the right time. You must learn to have the self-discipline to avoid the temptations of social media and the vast wonders of the internet and do what you need to do.

If you find this difficult, focus on the creation principle which provides a simple four-step process to ensure you finish what you start. First you think it then you speak it, then you act it and finally, you do it. Thinking a thing is easy but you must ensure you have the self-discipline to see ventures through. This is why speaking it can help as by putting the thoughts into words you are making yourself accountable in ensuring the task is completed.

By directing your self-discipline completely towards the concepts of creation you help to implement the harvest principle which elaborates on the idea that success is simply effort magnified by proper timing and bolster by a regular routine.

Practice gratitude: When we are grateful for things we have; we are less likely to satisfy that urge for instant gratification. It takes us a step away from always wanting more of what we don't have. Take the time to appreciate all those around you and even the little things that they do.

The benefits of gratitude are probably more than you might imagine. It has not only been able to boost your mental health, but it also encourages you to be more balanced emotionally, and spiritually. Gratitude, over time, helps to make you feel like you have an abundance even when you are living with limitations.

Conclusion

The next step is to delve into the world of self-love and self-care. You know that you need help to keep moving forward in the right direction. Otherwise, you would not have bought this book! Cognitive Behavioral Therapy is the most cutting-edge system of therapy available. It is, arguably, also the most effective. There is a reason why it has taken the United States by storm and earned its place as a top treatment plan for most psychologists today.

In fact, here are some great statistics about Cognitive Behavioral Therapy just to remind you of what a great system it is:

•It has been found CBT can be upwards of 75% effective as a single system.

•After about 8-15 sessions, 50-85% of those using it to battle anxiety and/or depression felt their symptoms were under control.

•Combining both chemical treatment (medication) and Cognitive Behavioral Therapy is the single most effective treatment method for long-term psychological disturbances.

Cognitive Behavioral Therapy is only half of the battle, however. You must also find it within yourself, to be honest with yourself and change your entire way of thinking. Cognitive Behavioral Therapy is hard- it is not an easy path to go down. You will find endless challenges as you put all of the tenants of this treatment plan into action. The point of it is to fight through and come out swinging.

Do not be discouraged at your first relapse. No matter what, you are worthy, and you will be okay. Relapse is, inevitably, a part of recovery. You have not failed just because you were not able to complete the steps in the allotted time. You may need just to take a step back and reframe how you are thinking about the process.

There are also many different ways to incorporate Cognitive Behavioral Therapy into your life. It is so incredibly easy to integrate into every day. You will be so much better off for it, too.

I would recommend that the first thing you do after reading this book is to invest in either a great workbook for Cognitive Behavioral Therapy or at least a blank journal. Even just keeping track of your moods can make all the difference. Even if that is the only lesson you take away from reading this book, I will be happy! Of course, it would also be nice if you began to think about your cognitive distortions. And if you put all of the exercises into practice. I know that some of them feel a little in-genuine or even "cheesy," but I promise that they will absolutely change your life.

You deserve to live a life of freedom and relaxation. You deserve consistent, strong relationships which you feel confident in. You deserve to feel like you are the one in the driver's seat. You deserve a great night of rest, easy interpersonal relationships, and to love the person you see in the mirror. Whether you read this as a way to help you fall asleep due to insomnia or to help you bring your panic attacks under control, there is a method in this book that will solve your problem.

As we conclude, it is essential to address the reason why you need to maintain your achievements. Achieving the gains is easy but we cannot say the same about maintaining them. It is common to think that once you have acquired what you are looking for, the benefits will stick in you magically and forever. From experience, thinking that way will make you fall back on what you solved sooner than you thought.

Therefore, the question you should ask yourself is this: how do you intend to keep the progress that you have developed so far? How many sessions do you need or how many times do you need to revisit the techniques offered in order to guarantee the longevity of what you have learnt?

Have a message that helps you stick to your values, such as 'Use it to live happier and less worried.' Such messages will help you every time you need to troubleshoot future events.

The only thing left to do is, well, to just do it!

BOOK 2 - Master your Emotions

Improve Your Control, Emotional Intelligence, Social Skills & EQ. Increase Your Freedom from Anger, Stress, Depression and Negativity. Management Mental Health and Feeling Guide

Daniel Mercer

Introduction

Emotions can be complex, because it can be difficult to understand just why they arise. Though many individuals look at the situation they are experiencing in the present moment to determine why they react emotionally, there are several other factors that can impact your emotions. Emotion can be the result of internal and external factors and the mind tends to use them as a defense mechanism to protect you from further uncomfortable feelings. This chapter will give you a deeper understanding of the root of your emotions and the main factors that can impact whether you experience more positive or negative emotions.

The difference between emotions and mood

Many think that emotions and mood are the same, or are at least commonly interchanged to express the same thing. Emotions and your mood do, however, have distinct differences. As discussed, emotions tend to be experienced over a short time. They can be intense, and there is always an identifiable trigger that causes these emotions to occur. Your mood, on the other hand, often describes a longer lasting state of mind or feeling. Moods may not be as intense, but it can be equally difficult to identify the cause. It can take days or longer to pinpoint the trigger for what is causing your mood, especially when it comes to more negative moods. Often, these are circumstances.

Moods and emotions can, however, be experienced at the same time. Even when you are in a negative mood, you can experience bouts of joy and happiness. Typically, your mood and emotions will reflect one another. So, if you are in a sad or depressed mood, you may feel emotions that are more anxious, sad, and even angry. Understanding this difference between mood and emotion will help you better identify what you are feeling, as well as better understand what triggers can cause these emotions to arise.

How the brain processes emotions

The way the brain operates can have a great impact on the emotions we feel, how intensely we experience these emotions, and our ability to process and work through them. Through a great deal of neurological testing and research, we've found that many areas of the brain can have an impact on emotions. When some of these areas are damaged or not function properly, it can be more difficult to control our emotions or interpret them correctly.

- The cerebrum part of the brain is where emotional control takes places and identifies how we relate to specific emotions

- The right hemisphere of the brain is where we process emotional expressions
- The frontal lobe of the brain allows us to process the complexities of emotions
- In the temporal lobes, we process the audio and visual perceptions from emotional responses
- The limbic system is where we access our survival emotions.

Additional sections of the brain may affect specific emotions such as fear and love, or also affect the emotional response in other areas of the brain.

The hypothalamus affects the limbic system and can impact emotional response as it regulates hormones.

The hippocampus is the section of the brain that is responsible for storing and retrieving memories. These memories can have an effect on how you respond to certain situations, and results in a repeat of emotional response when confronted with similar situations.

The amygdala is the main area of the brain that is said to process emotions. When you confront an external stimulus, this area of the brain helps decide the most appropriate way to respond to that factor. The amygdala also allows you to process the emotional response of others. Many suggest that this section of the brain is directly linked to our flight-or-fight response, when we feel fear or that we are in danger.

The limbic cortex is located in the prefrontal cortex, where we analyze abstract and cognitive perceptions in order to make sound judgments or decisions.

Additionally, certain areas of the brain directly control some of our basic emotions, such as fear, anger, happiness, and love.

CHAPTER 1 - WHAT ARE EMOTIONS?

There are varied definitions of emotions plus some existing literature attempts to compare emotions with feelings in a bid to justify which of both precedes the other. Taking all information and viewpoints into consideration, we can define emotions on three different levels.

•**Physically**: Feelings are reactions from the brain's subcortical sections in response to stimuli. These reactions generate biochemical responses within your body thus changing one's physical condition. They can in turn compel one to action on any matter that stirs the emotions in the threatening or enjoyable way. For this reason, they are seen as part of human survival instincts also.

•**Mentally**: Emotions are normal responses that provide rise to certain thoughts and circumstances of the mind, changing one's state of mind with regards to the stimuli. For this reason our thoughts are influenced by emotions before we can even think them often! It also dates back to remembering how someone or matter made you feel as the emotional memory space is stored for you to mentally think about down the road.

•**Emotionally**: This seems like an obvious one however the emotional component of emotions is usually oddly the hardest part for most people to grasp! It exists within us beyond the physical and mental elements somewhere. This is the primary of emotion itself; what we feel, how we experience, and the role these feelings play inside our lives. Simply, it is the overall emotional condition of being.

Feelings create an endless response cycle between your physical body and brain for better or worse. They can control your activities or help enhance them - this all depends on your personal relationship with them and your emotional state to be. Overall, feelings are responses to different circumstances that go far beyond the physical features of chemicals releasing within the body.

Emotional senses range between cheerfulness, shock, and anxiety, to sorrow, hatred, and rage. Although feelings are an important part of human living, they may affect your personal conduct and sometimes, you can risk attaching feelings to everything.

Although these skills are essential for the workplace, they will help you improve your relationships outside of work also. To build up, and perfect, your emotional intelligence you need to start paying even more attention to emotions, yours' and others', start to pay attention more and talk less, and make an effort to become more available to other people's viewpoint.

CHAPTER 2 - WHAT IS EMOTIONAL INTELLIGENCE?

Almost all of us know an emotionally intelligent person (if you're lucky, more than one maybe). He or she always seems to be saying the right things however tricky the situation. They have a way of "handling the situation" and preventing it from becoming negative or destructive. They know how to assert themselves without offending others. These folks are also more caring, sensitive, considerate, compassionate, and empathetic.

They don't allow emotions to swing their behavior. Emotionally intelligent people may not have the answers to all your problems but they have the ability to make you feel more positive and hopeful about a situation.

The term emotional intelligence was made popular by author psychologist, Daniel Goleman in 1995, though the term itself was created by Michael Beldoch during the mid-20th century. Emotional intelligence is the ability to monitor our and other people's feelings, differentiating between various emotions, naming feelings, and leveraging this invaluable emotion-based information for directing our actions, thoughts, behavior patterns, and decisions.

This illustrates emotional intelligence using broader or more general terms, though, there is a lot of debate within the socio-psycho scientific community about what emotional intelligence exactly is and what it includes. One component of emotional intelligence that everyone agrees with is that is an ability to recognize, understand, and manage our and other people's feelings.

The psychology of attachment mentions that our present emotional experiences can be traced to our early encounters with emotions. It can be overpowering emotions or feelings we experienced in our childhood or adolescent years that left a deep impact on us. Our present-day ability to deal with a variety of feelings such as unhappiness, joy, fear, anger, nervousness and more is closely linked to the nature of our early emotional experiences. If your emotions were identified, acknowledged, and valued during the early stages of psychological growth and development, they can become valuable assets. Likewise, if the experiences were more negative and painful, you may be conditioned to detach yourself from these feelings and emotions.

Emotional intelligence facilitates our connection with our emotions and helps us identify changing feelings whenever they occur. This is critical to regulating our thoughts, emotions, and actions.

Identifying and understanding our emotions is the key to controlling them. When we can predict how you are likely to feel in a particular situation, doesn't it become easier to manage your reaction beforehand? This allows us to think logically about a feeling before responding or reacting to it impulsively or involuntarily. We are no longer servants of our impulses and have higher control of our actions owing to greater awareness of our feelings and emotions. This prevents us from taking irrational, regretful, and destructive steps that we can harm our relationships in hindsight.

We also master the art of placing ourselves in other people's shoes by developing more empathy. This can be a huge asset in our personal and professional life. For example, if a worker is not putting his best effort, an emotionally intelligent manager will not simply assume the worker is being lazy or is not interested in working.

They will attempt to reach out to the individual and understand his/her reasons for not performing to the best of his/her abilities. The person may be afraid of making mistakes or he/she may be low on confidence about his/her abilities. Resolving people-related issues becomes easier when you can place yourself in someone else's shoes and think and feel things from their point of view.

The concept of emotional intelligence can be more complex than it appears, owing to the fact that naming emotions and feelings is no mean feat. Emotions registered in the subconscious and unconscious are often nameless, marked by an inability to comprehend their experience or understand them. There are far more emotions than words created in any language to express them. Also, emotions are often entwined into one another or overpowered by another mental state. For instance, fear may just be an overpowering desire to escape and can be fully experienced only in retrospect. Another aspect is that certain emotions are too painful to dwell upon, creating more complex emotions.

Emotional intelligence can be tricky because all emotions do not possess a convenient uniformity. Though our emotions are largely reflective of our values and refinement of those values, we can also feel emotions about an existing emotion. Sounds complicated? Ever felt guilty or shameful about envying someone? Yes, that's an emotion about feeling an emotion. While some emotions are transparent, others are hazier and more equivocal. For example, our love for higher virtues, such as truth, is experienced as intensely profound, while our resentment for an individual of accomplishments higher than ours leaves us feeling uncomfortable.

So, what is it about emotional intelligence that makes it the single largest predictive index for success at work? Goleman pointed out that emotional intelligence includes 67% of all abilities required for higher performance among leaders. It matters more than (twice as much to be precise) technical expertise or the conventional IQ. Other research points to the fact that general intelligence and ability are closely associated with leadership. As emotional intelligence is becoming more and more coveted by personality and behavior analysts, new markers of emotional intelligence and techniques of developing EQ are rapidly gaining popularity.

There are various emotional intelligence models such as the specific ability model that has noted ways through which emotions can facilitate better thoughts, behavior, and understanding. For instance, an individual who is more emotionally reactive to important issues will focus on those specific crucial facets of his life. Emotional facilitation factors also include knowing when to encompass or remove emotions from one's thoughts according to the context and circumstances. The model correlates to heightened emotional reasoning and a responsive understanding of people, situations, and the environment in everyday life.

Emotional intelligence filled a large gap in a rather strange finding, which concluded that individuals possessing average IQ outperformed those with high IQ in about 70% of all instances. This created a huge wrench into the existing belief people held of intelligence quotient being the single largest measure of a person's success. In 1995, research began to quickly identify emotional intelligence as a critical component for setting superstar performers apart from the average Joe pack.

Emotional intelligence consists of both personal and social competence. It affects our ability to manage behavior, negotiate social complexities, and exercise personal decisions which help us achieve greater positive results.

Personal competence consists of self-management and self-awareness that emphasizes more on your ability to interact with others. It is a person's individual competency in staying aware of their own emotions and managing their behavior and behavioral tendencies for optimal results. Self-awareness is one's ability to correctly perceive your own emotions and gain a better awareness of them when they happen, while self-management is the ability to use this awareness to manage your behavior for more positive results.

Social competence comprises of greater social awareness and social relationship management skills. It is an individual's ability to gain an intuitive understanding of other's moods, motives, and behavior for forging better relationships. Social awareness, under social competence, is all about correctly identifying emotions in others and trying to perceive what's really happening inside them. Relationship management, on the other hand, is the ability to utilize self-emotional awareness and understanding of other's emotions to manage social interactions successfully.

Personally, we can utilize our emotions to increase self-control and safeguard ourselves emotionally. It can also often be misused to gain complete control over others by manipulating their emotions to create feelings of fear, despair, and self-control. Psychologists and behavior experts, who emphasize the importance of emotional skills to enhance people's lives, do not sometimes take into consideration the ethical dimensions of having access to an individual's emotional make-up.

Emotional intelligence has a large impact on a number of sectors including the corporate world. Several firms use emotional intelligence assessments as part of their recruitment process. Studies have consistently pointed to the fact that people with evolved leadership skills tend to display greater emotional intelligence, revealing that well-developed EQ is a crucial characteristic for business leaders, supervisors leading big teams into performance, and future managers.

Politicians and advertisers harness the power of emotional quotient brilliantly to influence masses to make purchases or vote in their favor. Advertising agencies quite successfully manipulate emotions such as fear and aspirations to accomplish their client's objectives by using information about their target audience's emotions and how these emotions function for influencing voting or buyer behavior.

Emotional intelligence is distinct from one's intellect in the sense that it taps into the fundamental elements of human behavioral patterns. Also, there is no established connection between intelligence quotient and emotional quotient. You just can't predict an individual's EQ based on their smartness. Also, your IQ will be the same at age 15, as it will be at age 60. Emotional intelligence, on the other hand, will most likely evolve over the years according to practice and experiences. It is a more flexible set.

CHAPTER 3 - HOW TO IDENTIFY EMOTIONS

Emotions refer to the way you react to a situation. It is not an easy task doing so; it takes time and patience. Different people have different emotions, and you need to take time for you to identify the right emotion.

So, why should you even identify the emotions in the first place? Emotions come in three parts - the subjective, physiological, and expressive component. The subjective component refers to how you experience emotion while the physiological component refers to how the body reacts to the emotion while the expressive component refers to how you behave when you respond to the emotion. These elements play a big role in how you respond to emotion.

The Roles That Emotions Play In Our Lives

They Motivate Us to Take Action

The emotions dictate the way you react to the situation. For instance, when you are faced with an exam, you will feel anxious about how well you will perform and how the test will affect the results you get. Because of the responses, you might be forced to study better. The emotion allows you to take some action and improves the outcome. Emotions also allow us to decide which actions to take; usually, the actions are aimed at helping us to experience more positive emotions while we reduce the probability of negative emotions.

Emotions Help Us Survive

Emotions are a way for us to avoid danger, survive ad reproduce. When we get angry, the next natural reaction is to confront what is causing the irritation. When we are afraid, we will most likely run.

Emotions play the role of motivating us to take action quickly, something that will increase the chances of success and survival.

They Help Us Make Decisions

Emotions have the ability to influence the decisions that we make. For instance, when we get annoyed, we look for a way to change the situation. Even when we have situations that require us to decide purely by rationality and logic, we still work by emotions.

Emotions Help Us Communicate

When we communicate with other people, it is vital that we give them clues that will make them understand our situation better. These clues involve emotions that we then display through body language. This can be in the form of facial expressions that are connected to certain emotions that we experience.

In some cases, it can involve us stating how we feel directly. For instance, when we tell someone that we are sad, happy, or frightened, then we ate, giving them vital information that they can utilize to take action.

They Help Us to Understand Others

Just the way we give other people an idea of how we feel when we show them the emotions we go through, the emotions of other people also give us an idea of what other people are thinking or planning.

When we know how to identify and interpret emotions, we have the capacity to react to their emotions the right way. When we learn about emotions, we get to react the right way to them, which means more meaningful relationships with other people.

How to Recognize Emotions

For you to manage your emotions, you first need to learn how to identify them the right way. A significant percentage of the people try to ignore the emotional reactions, letting the emotions build up within them. When this happens, the result is impaired ability to use their emotions in a productive way.

Other people recognize the emotions but find it difficult to control them, and they find themselves at the mercy of the emotions.

For you to use your emotions the right way, you need first to identify the emotions the right way. Let us look at the best way to identify the emotions:

1. **Understand the Trigger**

The first step towards identifying the emotion is first to know what caused it. This will help you to describe the events that led to the emotional event. In this step, try to stick to facts alone.

You can write down the event that led to the emotion so that you have it clear in your mind.

2. **Why Do You Think It Happened?**

The next step is to identify the possible causes that led to the emotional event. This is crucial because it determines the meaning that you give to the situation that happened. The type of emotional event that led to the issue will determine the way you react to the event in question.

3. How the Situation Made you Feel

The next step is to determine how the emotional event made you feel both physically and emotionally. This will help you see whether the emotion resulted in a positive or negative reaction.

You need to notice both the positive as well as the negative emotional and physical reactions that you felt when it happened. Notice any physical feelings that you experience, such as tightness in the body.

4. What Was Your Reaction

You need to ask yourself this question so that you understand your urges. However, for the process to be effective, you need to make sure you are completely honest. It might be painful to admit some of the urges that you felt when the event happened. When we face some situations, we at times get strange urges to react differently. Some of the emotions that we go through might make us regret later on.

You need to compare your reaction at the moment that things happened and how you usually react normally. This will tell you whether you managed to control the urge or you failed to do so.

5. What Did You Do and Say?

The next step would be to understand what you actually said or did due to the emotions. Even though you didn't manage to respond the right way, you need to be honest with yourself about how you handled the situation. You also need to understand how the decision you made impacted on the situation. This can be a good learning experience for you.

Once you evaluate your reaction, you can then use the situation to learn how to handle another situation that might arise.

6. How Did the Reaction Affect You Later on?

The final step in identifying the emotions is to understand the consequences of the actions that you took. If you said some words during the event, how did they affect you? On the other hand, if you acted in a certain way, how did it affect you later on?

So, if you find yourself being overly attached to your emotions next time, you need to ask yourself what happened and take the time to observe how you react when it happens. Go through these steps so that you can recognize your emotions. Once you practice and get used to these steps, you will be able to identify your emotions the right way and then choose the best way to respond to situations.

CHAPTER 4 - MASTER YOUR EMOTIONS TOOLBOX

Mastering your emotions is accomplished when you decide you do not want to be controlled by the negativity you confront in your life. This requires dedication and commitment, but can be highly rewarding. When you learn to master your emotions, you are less likely to play the role of victim. Instead, you allow your emotions — the negative and the positive — to empower you. By developing your emotional intelligence skills, you have already laid the foundation to have complete control over your emotions. This can have a powerful impact on your success, relationships, health, and overall quality of life.

What makes mastering your emotions difficult is that we often automatically fall into negative thought patterns. Negative thoughts not only impact your emotional experience — they can completely dictate how you behave and react to emotional experiences, as well as determine which emotional experience you will have more of. By first understanding how these negative thought patterns affect your emotional health, you will be able to more clearly and intentionally shift your negativity to positive experiences and lessons.

How to change your emotional state from stressed and negative to positive and productive

As you can see, negative thoughts tend to be our default. They are often deeply rooted in our behaviors and outlook on life. One of the first things to do to adopt a more positive and productive state is to begin wiring your brain to search for the positives in each day. When you catch yourself having negative thoughts, opinions, or emotions, counter this with at least three positive emotional experiences. Up until now, you have wired your brain to seek out the negative — this is why it seems so easy to get caught up in the negativity. But by shifting the ratio of negative and positive experiences so that you have more enjoyable moments, it will become second nature and more natural to find these positive parts of your day.

Once you have gotten a better handle on actively searching for positive experiences, there are more steps you can take to shift your stressed out and negative emotional experience to ones that will serve you in a more productive and positive way.

Learn to express your emotions

It is one thing to understand your emotions, but it is another thing to admit to the emotions you are experiencing. Often, we secretly deal with our emotions in private, because there tends to be a negative connotation associated with extreme negative emotions. For this reason, your emotions still have control over you. When you allow your emotions to force you to hide, deny, or cover up what you are feeling, you are not fully addressing them.

When you learn to properly express your emotions, you learn how to take control of them — and to control them in a way that moves you in a more positive direction. In order to express your emotions properly, you need to first be able to identify what you are feeling in the present moment. Practice properly expressing the emotion you are experiencing by stating these emotions out loud. When you announce these emotions, do so with confidence and empowerment. Stating your emotions to yourself out loud when you are alone will help you build confidence so you can properly state them out loud in front of others. When you feel comfortable enough, practice stating your emotions out loud to people you trust and feel safe with. You can begin this practice by focusing just on expressing your more positive emotions, and then begin to express your emotions when you are in more challenging situations. Remember that when you openly state your emotions, you are inviting others to do the same, and they may not feel the same way you do. Keep an open mind and remain confident about what you are feeling — don't let what others say sway you from your own experiences.

Tracking your emotions

One of the best ways to begin identifying how you handle stressful and negative situations is to keep track of them. Starting an emotional, or mood journal can help you better organize, understand, and change your negative thought patterns, behaviors, and emotional responses. Begin keeping a daily log of everything you experience throughout your day. How did you feel in each significant moment, and what were your thoughts as you were going through the motions?

When you do this daily over a long period of time, you will begin to take notice of some of your emotional patterns. You can clearly identify triggers that cause you to feel more negatively. This also allows you to pinpoint the thoughts that occur as you have emotional experiences. This simple exercise, which can be done in five or ten minutes, can help you strengthen your self-awareness.

Not only will journaling about your emotions allow you to change your negative experiences into positive ones, but the process can also be beneficial for your mental health. Getting these things out of your head can help reduce your risk of suffering from depression and anxiety. This is because you are not just keeping the experience stuck in your head and dwelling on one aspect of the event, which tends to be just the negative. When you write it down, you can clearly see what caused you to have such a negative reaction. This can then allow you to find a better way of dealing with situations like these in the future.

Take care of yourself

How you treat yourself can have a major impact on how you handle negative situations. As you learned earlier, the way you treat yourself impacts your confidence, and when you lack confidence, it will be more difficult to overcome your negative thought patterns. When you treat yourself with kindness and compassion, you're able to better confront negative situations and stress in a more calm and proactive way. In order to shift from constantly thinking things are stressful and negative, you want to be able to treat yourself in a way that allows you to make mistakes, take risks, and find solutions.

This is especially important when it comes to how you talk to yourself. If you find that your internal dialogue is one that constantly berates you, points out your failures, or keeps you feeling stuck and incapable, you need to first focus on shifting this negative mindset. A negative thought process will never allow you to see the positive in any situation, whether it is a joyful or unpleasant one.

Reframe your perspective

There are a number of ways to shift your perspective to better cope and to find the positive in most negative situations. You can begin by taking on a more positive outlook. Instead of being discouraged, hurt, or angry by a specific experience, learn to identify how the situation has healed you and allowed you to grow. You can also shift your perspective by looking at where you will be years from now. Many bad experiences are stressful and negative at the moment. Recall an event that you thought was the worst thing that could ever happen to you. Do you still have those same negative emotions? Chances are, you can probably look back and laugh at yourself for ever thinking that way. Before you begin to think about how bad a situation is, remember to look ahead and consider how you will view this situation in the future. Additionally, you can begin to understand your own worst-case perspective. This allows you to truly see the situation is not as bad as you are making it seem. To better utilize this shifting perspective, you want to identify the positive around each negative situation. You will begin to realize that there are plenty of things to be motivated and feel good about, despite things not turning out exactly how you had hoped.

You can also try taking an empathetic perspective to shift your attitude to a more positive and productive one. This type of perspective shifting provides you with the opportunity to see things from someone else's point of view. Many times, we can be so caught up in our own experience that we fail to recognize the other people around us and how they may be interpreting the same situation differently. When you take the time to look at things from another person's point of view, you can gain an understanding of how to let go of your own hurt feelings, resentment, and negative emotions to truly embrace the positives that are present.

Practice forgiveness

Forgiveness can provide you with a number of benefits, especially when it comes to accepting negative events. When you forgive yourself and others for any negativity, you will reduce your emotions of hurt, anger, and disappointment. Forgiveness is simply the act of acknowledging what occurred and letting it go so it does not have a greater negative effect on you.

Regaining positive emotions

It can seem impossible to experience positive emotions to the fullest extent when you have spent so much time allowing the negative ones to control your life. When this occurs, your brain is programmed to seek out more negative experiences, as this is what it is currently wired to do. When you want to attract more positive experiences your way, you need to first focus on retraining your brain to find them.

It can be easy to become overwhelmed by negative emotions, and these can quickly spiral into a state of mind that leaves you feeling lost and out of control. When you begin to notice you are feeling stuck, chronically stressed, and indecisive, there are simple steps that can help you have more positive experiences.

Ask yourself a lot of questions

Question what you are feeling, why you are feeling that way, what has occurred in your past that could be triggering your emotional response, and if the way you are behaving in reaction to these emotions causes you to look at these emotions in an adaptive or maladaptive way? Analyzing your emotions, the situation, and your behavior is one of the first ways you can begin to experience more positive emotions. Once you have answered these questions, you can use your answers to help you visualize better solutions. When you want to change your negative emotions to more positive ones, visualizing can allow you to clearly develop a specific solution for dealing with emotions.

Get involved in more healthy activities

Keeping your body healthy affects your emotional health, just as your emotional health affects your physical health. When you take the time to take care of yourself, you feel better about yourself, which results in more positive emotions. Find activities that make you feel good — this can include starting a new hobby, listening to music, being creative, and practicing physical activity.

Often, these types of activities can be combined, such as exercising while listening to uplifting music or finding a hobby that also allows you to be creative like painting, photography, or learning to play an instrument. Pushing yourself to try new things helps build your confidence, and when you have more confidence, you feel more in control and able to handle difficult situations.

Socialize and be available for others

When you know there is a situation, event, or encounter coming up that you recognize as something that will leave you feeling negative, talking with others can help in a number of ways. Reaching out to your support group can give you a new perspective on the upcoming situation, as well as provide you with positive feedback about how to handle it. Being social can also help reduce the stress and anxiety you may be feeling about the situation, because your support group can help you look at things realistically.

Aside from turning to your support system, when you make yourself more available to others, you can learn to strengthen your empathy. Opening up yourself to be supportive to others who are going through difficult times can bring you more awareness of how others respond to difficult situations and this, in return, can help you gain a better awareness of your own responses.

Improve your attitude

Attitude, like emotions, can impact many areas of your life. Where your emotions involve your reaction toward the things you encounter in your life, attitude is how you approach your day and life experiences. Your attitude can have a serious impact on your emotions. When you constantly approach things with a negative view, your emotions will reflect this view, leading to more negative experiences. Emotions are more challenging to control, because you have little choice over which emotions you will experience, and you can really only control how you react to these emotions. Attitude, however, is a choice. You can fully decide how you will approach things in your life. You have full control over whether you think the worst or choose to believe that everything happens for a reason and are able to find the lesson instead of just seeing the setbacks.

Attitude can always be improved. Improving your attitude can result in better emotional experiences. Still, on especially trying days, keeping a positive attitude can be a challenge. These simple actions can help turn your attitude around.

Do your best and let go

Your attitude can be greatly affected by things out of your control. Unfortunately, we often focus on the aspects we have no control over. Did you get the job or not? Did you pass your final exam? Did you win the bid on your dream home? What will your boss think of the latest project you completed for work? All of these situations can go one of two ways, and often, we spend a great deal of time worrying about the outcome. When you are confronted with situations like these, do what you can to increase the chances of things going the way you want them to. You can spend extra time preparing for your job interview, study for the exam, do your research on the home and area you want to buy in, and give 100 percent on your project. All you have control over is your own actions. If you have done your best, there is no point in stressing about the outcome and letting this bring down your attitude, as this will only lead to emotions being more anxious, more fearful, more stressful, and more frustrating. When you learn to accept that you have done your best and let go of what may or may not happen, you can improve your attitude and focus on the positive.

Surround yourself with others who have a positive attitude

Just as with your emotions, the people you spend the most time with will affect your attitude, as well. If the people you surround yourself with tend to have a more negative attitude and approach to life, yours will often be the same. If you want to have a more positive attitude, you'll want to take a close look at the people you spend the most time with. Do they tend to be more optimistic? Do they view things from a more positive perspective? If not, there is a good chance you want to reevaluate how much time you spend with them. People who have a more positive attitude tend to be more encouraging, supportive, and inspiring, and these are the people you want to spend more time with if you want to improve your attitude.

Keep your actions in line with your values

When you live your life with more purpose, you will live your life with a more positive attitude. So often, we go through life simply performing mundane actions, which can lead to an attitude that is hopeless, uninspired, and lacks motivation. When you find more purpose in life, you tend to take a different approach to your daily activities.

Having your own set of values and purpose will also keep you from comparing your life to others'. Many times, we see someone else's life and think we need to live the same way and have the same things. Comparing yourself to others in this way can lead to you viewing life with a negative attitude, keeping you feeling as though you are less than or not equal to others. When you have recognized your purpose, you avoid shifting your focus to trying to obtain what others have instead of what will bring you more joy. Remember, most of what we see of someone's life is what they allow us to see. There is no way to know how this person actually lives. They may have plenty of materialistic things, but this doesn't mean they have the things that truly make up a happy life. Focus on the things that will bring your life more happiness and ask if those things align with your purpose. Doing this will help you maintain a more positive attitude.

Practice mindfulness

Most people rush through their day constantly thinking about what needs to be done next or dwelling on the things they haven't yet done or will have the time to do. Living this way keeps you in a place or worry, anxiety, and stress. Your attitude is often detached from the current situation, as you are always focusing on something else. Mindfulness helps you pause the chaos and frantic motions of the day and allows you to gain control over the present moment.

By stopping to become aware of what is happening in the here and now, you will bring more peace and calm into your life. Practicing mindfulness daily can help you align your attitudes and actions in a more positive direction. Spend at least ten minutes a day just focusing on your thoughts. Take note of your internal dialogue and what you are saying to yourself about what you need to get done. If you notice the words you use are more negative or cause you to feel more anxiety or stress, shift your thinking to use more positive and encouraging language. By pausing for this brief amount of time, you can check in with yourself and acknowledge what your body is feeling and how your thoughts are impacting your attitude. Being more mindful is a highly beneficial way to reduce your stress, anxiety, and negative thoughts. Practicing mindfulness regularly can help improve your attitude as well as give you a better insight on your emotional responses on a daily basis.

Express more gratitude

Gratitude is your ability to recognize and appreciate all you have in your life. This includes the people you encounter, the material things you have obtained, the experiences you have lived through, and all the other small details that often go unnoticed in your day. Being grateful is one of the easiest ways you can significantly change your attitude.

As soon as you wake in the morning, spend time being grateful for a new day, and be thankful for all that you will encounter that day and the lessons you will learn. Spend time at the end of each day writing down at least three specific things you are grateful for that day. When you begin to feel stressed, pause and look at the situation. What can you find to be grateful about in that moment? When you express more gratitude for all you have, you invite more good to come your way. Practicing gratitude on a daily basis also improves your attitude, because you begin to look at your day with a sense of already having all you need. You eliminate your feelings of lacking or need and increase your feelings of love and fulfillment.

CHAPTER 5 - EMOTIONAL INTELLIGENCE AND OUR EMOTIONS

How to interpret, understand and utilize our emotions

Observe Your Feelings throughout the Day

Practice observing and identifying your feelings all day. How do certain experiences at various points in time during the day make you feel? When people say something that angers you, carefully note what exactly they've said to trigger the feeling of anger. This will help you develop a wide range of emotional vocabulary. I would even go a step further and say, for the purpose of quickly and easily identifying them, give your emotions names.

Labeling emotions makes it easier to identify specific emotions because even emotions like anger can have several different forms. For instance, it can be anger out of humiliation or anger induced by a feeling of jealousy or anger owing to expectations that are not met.

Practice Deep Breathing and Mindfulness

All our emotions are experienced physically. When we are angry, upset or stressed, the feelings manifest themselves through our body. Our bodies respond on an evolutionary level (instinctively or involuntarily) like they would respond to a natural threat. Some physiological reactions to our emotions can be a speeding heartbeat, increased pulse rate, sweating, shallow breathing and more.

Question Your Perspective

The first step towards increasing your emotional intelligence and social skills is recognizing that there are multiple ways of looking at a situation. Even though you may completely believe that your perspective or way of looking at things is right, get into the habit of considering it from different angles rather than giving in to knee-jerk responses.

When you are angry or upset with someone, avoid reacting impulsively. Instead, slow down and consider various ways of explaining the circumstances. What are the different ways to explain the situation? Of course, you may still stick to your perspective but at least attempt to look at it from various angles before considering the situation in a calmer and more rational manner. At best, even if your perspective about the situation doesn't change, you'll get more time to calm down and think of a more positive, constructive response.

Celebrate Positive Emotions to Attract More of Them

Emotionally intelligent folks who experience greater positive energy lead more fulfilling relationships and are more resilient when it comes to responding to negative situations. Therefore, get into the habit of intentionally doing things that induce a sense of happiness and joy within you.

Know Yourself like No One Else

The epicenter of emotional intelligence is knowing yourself like no one else. Self-awareness is the key to developing greater emotional intelligence. Having a good understanding of your core characteristics, strengths, weaknesses, beliefs, values, attitude and other similar aspects of your personality helps you understand your positive and negative triggers.

Solicit Feedback and Constructive Criticism

One of the best ways to gain greater self-awareness is to obtain feedback from trusted friends and family members. Ask people whom you've known for a long time to give you honest, genuine and constructive feedback about your strengths and areas of development.

You may agree or disagree with them, but you'll get a good idea about the effect your emotions and actions have on others, thus shielding you from blind spots. You will recognize the effect your behavior has on others whether you intend to create that effect or not. Sometimes, even we are unaware of the effect we have on others.

Avoid Judgmental Emotions

Every emotion you feel is valid, even the seemingly negative ones. When we are judgmental about our emotions, it inhibits our ability to fully experience these emotions. Thus we are unable to use our emotions in positive, constructive ways. Rather than seeing them as negative or positive, view your emotions as information pieces that are closely linked to things happening within and around you.

How to interpret, understand and utilize other emotions

Let Go of Your Pride

Don't let pride or ego get in the way of you being able to manage relationships effectively. These two traits are going to be barriers and prevent you from empathizing the way that an emotionally intelligent person would. If you want to learn how to manage someone else's emotions successfully, you will have to start by tossing ego and pride out the window. Don't let stubbornness get in the way of being able to see the bigger picture. Learn to see things from their point of view, and ask yourself why they are reacting this way and what you can do to make the situation better. This helps you strengthen your empathizing skills and teach you how to handle similar situations in the future. To successfully manage someone else's emotions, you may have to be the bigger person.

Don't Judge

One of the most important steps in learning how to manage others is to listen to them without being judgmental. It may be a challenge, but you need to not let your personal biases or preferences get in the way of the situation. To effectively manage someone else's emotions, you must deal with it with an open mind. Don't come into the situation with preconceived notions of what you think is right or wrong, or how you think they should be. What you think may work for you, but it won't necessarily be the best solution for them.

Let Them Have Their Space

If needed, allow that person to have their space. Sometimes that could be the best thing to do, depending on the situation. Or encourage them to talk to you and let it all out. For example, if the person you are trying to help is crying as part of their emotional response, let them. They may be in need of an outlet to release all that pent-up emotion before they can begin to feel better. If they need some space for a couple of minutes, let them. What you basically need to do in this situation is be the missing support system that they need to feel better. That is how you help them manage their emotions effectively.

Identify Their Emotions

This is where your skills of self-awareness and empathy are going to help you out. When the person you're trying to handle is just one big emotional mess, you need to step in and be the objective one. Observe them and use your empathy skills to begin identifying what emotions they are displaying. Gauge the way that they may be feeling. When you can successfully identify the emotions that you're dealing with, you will be able to think of more effective solutions because you know what you're dealing with.

Ask Questions

The more questions that you ask, the more information you receive. The more information you receive, the better the solution you can come up with. Open-ended questions which encourage the person to talk and reveal more information is the best approach. You need to get a clear picture of what you're dealing with so that you can identify the problem, then plan the appropriate response or solution. Essentially, you need to get that person to reveal their story. There is always a reason why they are emotionally that way, and it is up to you to try and pinpoint what the cause is if they cannot help themselves.

Be Okay With Apologies

If at any point during the course of your interaction you may have done or said something that makes the other person feel worse, be okay with apologizing. When you have to manage someone else's emotions, it is not the time to be too proud to say that you are sorry, even if you believe you are right. You need to keep the peace, be the level-headed one in this situation, and once again be the bigger person. Be ready and willing to sincerely apologize if the situation calls for it.

CHAPTER 6 - CAN EMOTIONAL INTELLIGENCE BE DEVELOPED?

Indeed emotional intelligence can be learned and developed. One of the ways of enhancing your emotional intelligence is to observe how you react to other people. You should not rush to judgment before you comprehend all of the facts. Avoid stereotyping, people like this breed biases and clogs your judgment. Examine closely on the manner in which you interact with other people and try to empathize with them. Start being more open and accept the views of other people and needs. Then examine your workplace and determine if you seek attention for your accomplishments. While humility is a wonderful attribute, it does not imply that you lack self-confidence. Learn to give others a chance to shine by putting the focus on them and avoid worrying much about looking for praise.

It is possible to develop emotional intelligence by doing self-evaluation. Start by determining your weaknesses by responding to the question of are you willing to acknowledge that you are not perfect and that you need to fix some areas to become a better person. Muster the courage to examine yourself honestly as this can change your life. Then review how you respond to demanding situations. Some of the things to look out for could be that you get upset each time there is a delay or something does not conform to your plans. Review if you tend to get angry or blame others even when it is not their fault. Remember that the ability to remain composed and in charge of challenging situations is highly valued. Learn to maintain your emotions under control when things seem uncontrollable.

It is also important that you learn to take responsibility for your actions. For instance, apologize when you hurt the feelings of another person directly. Do not overlook what you did or seclude the person. If you make an honest attempt to rectify things, people are more willing to forgive and forget. Review how your actions will impact others prior to taking these actions. Put your place in the position of others if your decision will affect others. Ask yourself if you would prefer the same experience that you are about to subject others to and all this is part of operationalizing emotional intelligence.

Furthermore, begin to notice how you are feeling at any instance as a way of developing emotional intelligence. For instance, maintain a diary of the times that you are in a good mood at work. Understand that moods are contagious and that leaders of an organization define the weather in that organization. Ask yourself the kind of forecast that you are inviting at your workplace each day. By noticing when you are in a positive or negative mood, you will begin to handle your emotions. You can pause before reacting. Go further and imagine a performance conversation with your employee if you were in a negative state of mind and make a comparison to when having the same exchange when in a positive state of mind. Determine what would change. Desirably, start working to change your emotional state by taking a walk, listening to music, venting to a co-worker, or taking some deep breaths. You can also engage in any other action that assists you to avoid getting emotionally-charged.

Indeed your Emotional Intelligence is Not Rigid

While changing reputation might be relatively easier, adjusting the internal emotional intelligence tends to be difficult. In other words, there is a likely mismatch between the inside feelings and the external feelings a person projects to the people around him. It is acceptable that some individuals are born shy and self-centered while other persons are gifted with composure and soft-skills. Fortunately, every human behavior is adjustable. Another encouraging piece of news is that emotional intelligence increases with age, even where there are minimal interventions.

Effective Coaching Programs Work

Fortunately, a well-formulated intervention program will help an individual attain as much as 25% with respect to improving emotional intelligence. The most trainable element of emotional intelligence is interpersonal skills that can give 50% improvements. In this aspect, emotional intelligence can be treated as teaching social etiquette and negotiation. Stress management programs can yield as high as 35% improvement where both the trainer and the candidate are committed. Various studies affirm that with sufficient coaching, individuals can become more altruistic, pro-social, and compassionate. High emotional intelligence attributes are likely to lead to enhanced levels of mental and physical health as well as happiness. Improved marital relationships and social relationships are also attributed to enhanced emotional intelligence levels. The emotional intelligence programs can be more sophisticated and employ an eclectic approach

Seek Accurate Feedback

Agreeably, you can only work on your shortcomings if you get accurate feedback. Even though several inputs are critical for an effective training program, the most critical element is giving candidates accurate feedback. As seen, most individuals are unaware of how others perceive them and this common among managers. Your notion of how appealing you are is likely to be less accurate, and this attributed to overconfidence or wishful thinking. Most individually wrongly think that they are better than they actually are. For this reason, a good emotional intelligence training program should start with helping people comprehend what their real weaknesses and strengths are. The best outcomes can be realized by using reliable and valid evaluation methods, such as personality tests.

Concerning feedback, it is important that you deliberately create an environment and personality that encourages others to voice their opinions on you. Naturally, we all want to hear positive descriptions of our behaviors and personality. Feedback is not a criticism but rather a reflection of other people to us. Against this backdrop, it is critical that you do not attempt to disagree or victimize colleagues that voice feedback that portrays your weakness. A mistake that most individuals make is to interrupt the feedback and start justifying why they acted in the manner noted. Feedback is the complete picture that you painted out there, and the crowd is simply describing that picture.

Techniques Vary in Efficacy

In trying to enlist for coaching to improve your emotional intelligence levels appreciates that some techniques are more effective compared to others. Even though there is little evidence on the personal attributes of effective trainers, there is evidence of the approaches employed that deliver. Some interventions to improve emotional intelligence deliver more than others. Most of the high impact approaches to enhance emotional intelligence fall under cognitive-behavioral therapy. Efforts to improve psychological flexibility, which is the ability to acknowledge and handle challenging situations, are also effective. Meditation and relaxation are among the popular but not necessarily effective approaches to improving emotional intelligence levels. Interventions are created to improve self-esteem rarely deliver even though the popular belief is that they work. Additionally, coaching is also an art, and the effectiveness of a program will also rely on the talent of the trainer.

Similarly, some individuals are more trainable compared to others

It is highly possible for the best training methods for improving emotional intelligence levels to fail with particular individuals, and this is expected. There are unenthusiastic candidates. Clients with people skills, greater self-awareness, and more empathy are likely to be highly receptive to efforts to adjust their emotional intelligence levels. Individuals that are sensitive to criticism, worry about the future and are insecure should be willing to change for better emotional intelligence levels. Arguably, evaluating the candidates' trainability levels can enhance the impact of the training. Some studies link employee demoralization, and mental health issues to the behavior of their managers, and these inhibit productivity and employee retention levels. Most of the employee turnovers are triggered by stress. There is a possibility that managers embracing emotional intelligence training may lead to lessening the frequency of employee demoralization at the workplace.

Learn to Reduce Negative Emotions

Equally important, an individual should learn to manage adverse emotions that can overwhelm and impact the judgment. One of the ways of managing negative feelings is to change how you react to them. For instance, avoid making a negative conclusion outright when feeling strongly opinionated about the behavior of someone. Take an example where you feel that your friend is ignoring you for not picking your call. You can also take the position that your friend is busy or far from the phone, or the phone could be on silent mode. By avoid personalizing the behaviors of others, you will start to make an objective conclusion. Understand that a person acts or behaves because of the individual needs compared to the needs and feelings of others. By widening the perspective, one can lessen the possibility of misunderstanding.

Additionally, learning to minimize the fear of rejection and one proper way to handle the fear of rejection is to grant you multiple choices in critical situations. When you have several options, you will focus less on the outcome as you have alternatives. It is a good practice to be hopeful, but you must have contingency plans. For instance, when applying for a dream job, you are likely to be devastated if that was your only option if you are not absorbed. You can increase your options in the example given by applying for three exciting positions.

Learn to Stay Calm

The ability to maintain composure can help manage stress. The manner in which we handle stress can make the difference between being reactive and assertive. The most advisable thing to exercise when under duress is to maintain calmness.

Express Difficult Emotions and Be Assertive

It is sometimes necessary to define boundaries in life to communicate your stand. One of the situations that require taking a stand is when exercising the right to disagree or rejecting something without feeling remorseful, defining your priorities and safeguarding yourself from harm and duress.

Learn to Recover from Adversity

Accept that life is not straightforward, and mistakes and losses will arise. Additionally understand that the manner we think, act and feel in relation to challenges in life can create the difference between despair versus hope as well any other feelings. However, take each challenging situation as a learning moment. For instance, interrogate yourself on any benefits for thinking outside the preset boundaries, and you might realize you are likely to increase your choices and open up your feelings.

Learn to Express Intimate Emotions in Relationships

Another way of developing emotional intelligence is to possess the ability to express and validate loving emotions to maintain close personal relationships. With time you will learn to reciprocate constructive emotions and react positively when others return the feelings. One of the simple things that most people ignore is salutations and asking about how other people feel. From the adjectives that a person uses, you can effectively differentiate how the person is feeling and adjust your tone and attitude to be accommodative and comforting to the person. In addition, the body language bidding is important, and this includes things like smiling, eye contact and patting the elbow.

By learning to manifest positive emotions in a relationship, you enable the other person to return such reactions. Fortunately, positive emotions in a relationship and how to express them can be learned. One of the ways of enhancing your expression of positive emotions in a relationship is through the appropriate use of non-verbal cues of communication. For instance, project your voice when speaking about a formal issue and lower the pitch of your voice when talking about a personal issue. For some people shaking hands signals more than just greetings as it shows confidence and willingness to hold a conversation.

Without expressing your emotions, the other party in the relationship will not get a chance to read your feelings and this will interfere with communication. Words and phrases such as "I care about you" help verbalize your feelings. Some individuals find it embarrassing or feel unease expressing their true feelings. Lack of manifesting your true feelings will only increase the chances of misunderstanding between you and others. In a relationship, lack of expression of feelings can strain and end the relationship as each party cannot effectively read the mood and intentions of the other party creating a disconnect in communication and feelings.

Empathy

In addition to empathy, it is important also to visualize why the other person is happy or angry. Empathy should not be used only for negative emotions, such as anger and disappointment. It is also advisable to try and picture yourself as the other person who is contended or happy. By learning to position yourself in the other person's shoes, you will increase your understanding of the other person life. A mistake that most eager learners of emotional intelligence make is to consider empathy only for negative emotions such as anger and disappointment. Negative emotions are only a portion of the complete spectrum of human feelings, which include positive emotions.

Exercise

a. Do you agree that emotional intelligence can be learned and applied?

b. What do you consider are major barriers to you manifesting negative emotions?

c. Emotions are a form of energy, and it is important to dissipate the energy rather than bottling it up. Do you agree with this statement? Why?

d. Which leader or actor do you admire for the rare ability to remain calm even when viciously attacked during a debate? Which leader do you know will even walk away from a debate due to colleagues or the panel asking uneasy questions?

CHAPTER 7 - MANAGING EMOTIONS

The first thing we must do to improve our Emotional Intelligence is to adopt the habit of observing our reactions and behaviors. For this, it is essential to categorize in our mind some of the most habitual emotions especially those that we consider as negative or toxic, always under the premise of not condemning them or judging us for feeling them, since they do not have to be toxic in themselves. They can be considered as mere energy, and it is in our hands to channel it so that we can manage our emotions positively.

Example using Emotional Intelligence

Observing our emotions

Juan has to do an exhibition in public, when in the first he did a while ago he did not do too well. That makes her feel emotions like anxiety, anguish, or frustration. However, before the blood reaches the river, Juan stops for a moment. Take a deep breath to be more serene and observe those past experiences that are conditioning you to feel those emotions.

Accepting emotions

After his moment of reflection, Juan realizes that it is normal to feel that way. The other times that he had to expose in public, he did not feel prepared to do it for not having prepared well those exhibitions. However, now he is going to talk about a subject that he likes and that he masters perfectly, which makes him feel motivated to overcome his fears, provoking that these negative or toxic emotions are understood and accepted as part of a past that does not have to materialize in the present moment.

Managing emotions towards positive ends

After observing and accepting his emotions, Juan realizes that all this energy is making him live a very intense moment which leads him to imagine how happy he will feel about breaking down those barriers that until now were weighing on his successes. Transforming all that energy into enthusiasm, he is aware that nerves will continue to have them because he faces a significant challenge. But positively accept those nerves. Thinking that they will help you be more alert to meet your goal.

What would have happened without emotional intelligence?

If in the previous example, Juan had not managed his emotions, he would most likely have fallen into the clutches of negative thoughts. Imagining all kinds of repercussions for a possible failure, feeding this anxiety that in it was normal. Maybe to the point that would have been unattainable for him who in turn could have materialized in an exhibition in public with an insecure nonverbal language, instead of one that conveyed enthusiasm being able to stay blank no matter how well prepared the subject was.

Identify negative emotions

Identifying 9 emotions whose knowledge of their characteristics will help us control those emotions since our mind will have the ability to synthesize them into smaller parts.

That is, the more we know about each emotion, the less we will see them as something gross and abstract, but as steps, we can take.

Think of this metaphor: surely a mathematical integral that occupies a whole page made you very afraid to see it for the first time. But once they explained it to you and you saw that its resolution was part of a s of smaller continuous steps that fear was disappearing. Put another way; we are unable to climb a whole mountain at once. However, we are perfectly capable of walking several trails and climbing a few stretches of rock one after the other.

In this way we will go, for example, to think that we are angry and out of control (the raw result of emotions), to think that we feel anger because they have insulted us. Wondering if it deserves that we give so much value to that offense as to allow us to embitter the present moment, and it is that as the most spiritual authors defend, the conscience heals by itself.

9 negative emotions that you must learn to manage

1. Frustration

Frustration is one of the most important emotions to improve emotional intelligence. This makes us feel frustrated or disappointed with unfulfilled longings, desires, or goals. That is to say; we feel frustrated when we are not in a situation where we would like to be associating those feelings of an emotional slump with the circumstances that caused them. Their characteristics are:

- It causes anguish and can encourage us to avoid the situations that generated it.
- We tend to judge ourselves negatively damaging our self-concept.
- We blame others for not being in the situation we would like as a result of our defense mechanism.

- It is difficult for us to feel motivated in the face of new situations or challenges, no matter how different they are from those that caused us frustration.
- It encourages the exaltation of emotions such as jealousy, anguish, or shame.

2. Shame

Shame is an emotion that restrains us, undermining the confidence we need to do what we want. It causes a kind of paralysis effect, being considered by emotional intelligence as a parasite to develop our full potential. Their characteristics are:

- Constant projection towards what they can think of us.
- Beliefs of the subject that there is something bad or deficient in him.
- The tendency to avoid giving your opinions or making yourself known as it is.
- His constant repairs make him lose sight of the opportunities.
- Acts conditioned by shame usually do not fit with the talent or real abilities of individuals.
- Severe tendency to postpone the things that give her shame, never-ending them.
- Inclinations to abandon what they have learned for fear of being ridiculed.

3. Rejection

Rejection becomes toxic when we become obsessed with seeking acceptance from others. We need to control this emotion so that the value we give to ourselves is not subordinated to the opinions of others. That is, we have to learn to value ourselves from the inside for what we are. Let's see some of its characteristics:

- Constantly seek the approval of others and depend on their support to affirm themselves.
- Show off what you have for fear of rejection.
- Try to keep the rest of the people under control.

- Easily offended by negative ones and being able to respond with anger to them.
- Overestimate the opinions of others by becoming susceptible to them.
- Do not enjoy what you have if you do not receive a social value from it.
- The tendency to reject others as a result of frustration.

4. Fear

Fear is a healthy and usual emotion that drives us away from dangers. However, we often need to manage it so that this feeling of anguish does not prevent us from facing difficulties with confidence. According to Emotional Intelligence, fear becomes toxic when it paralyzes us even though we have the necessary resources to overcome it. Going back in this irrational way.

Exaggerated and circular imagination of all kinds of possible negative consequences.

· It amplifies all other emotions, both positive and negative.

· It paralyzes or accelerates and increases our abilities to remember those moments in which it acted.

· Forms patterns of behavior based on past experiences: "My ex-partner already deceived me, and now I do not trust anyone."

· It makes us concentrate too much on the past. We lose sight of the novelties of the present.

· It has a retroactive nature: "If I'm afraid of having sex for any reason, I start to get scared to meet someone I like, I'm afraid to kiss another person for the first time, connect sexually with her, etc.... The phases before a future fear are conditioned, generating fear in them as well.

· Reproduce mentally traumatic experiences over and over again with great detail. It is generating non-existent fears that can end up materializing in phobias.

5. Anger or anger

Getting angry is not always bad. Sometimes it can encourage our spirit of improvement and motivate us to change things. It increases our capacity to face adverse situations (resilience). Other times it helps us to realize our mistakes. The problem comes to us when those annoyances are caused by irrelevant reasons and without which we can extract anything positive in return. Or worse still, when they make us destroy what we had.

· It usually occurs when our expectations are not met.

· It diminishes our ability to be empathetic and assertive.

· It manifests itself in different levels, being able to be managed in different ways. Some release it little by little as it arrives. Others contain it and end up bursting at the least opportune moments. Others release it with forgiveness or meditation as they arrive...

· It can be materialized in violence when levels of frustration are high.

· It affects differently depending on the type of personality of each subject. It is usually more common in very competitive people or with a tendency to compare.

· His verbal responses can be passive (when it is contained), assertive (when it is managed) or aggressive (when given free rein).

It usually produces feelings of guilt. Aggravating the problem or raising the awareness of the person to manage this emotion better and even taking her to ask for forgiveness.

A trick that I usually use when I feel I am getting angry is to ask myself questions that invite me to reflect. I often ask myself: Does getting angry cause me something, or will it just make me feel bad? Is Will getting upset to encourage me to get something positive in the future? Can this anger help me in some way to enjoy my current or future more?

6. Jealousy

According to the theories on emotional intelligence, we produce jealousy when we are afraid of losing someone. It is commonly said that we can be jealous of another person because of what he or she has, but in those cases, we would be talking about a different emotion: envy.

· They affect a relationship between two people until it becomes toxic if the jealousy is high.

· They inhibit our feeling of feeling natural and free. What paradoxically encourages us to look for the adventure that we wanted to avoid.

· They return to those who suffer excessively controllers or strategists.

· They create exalted and distorted images about what the desired person can bring.

· It can materialize in gender violence.

· It can prevent us from appreciating and enjoying the present moment with the other person.

· Generates dictatorial attitudes where the affected person intrudes on everything and tries to direct it.

· Create illusory threats by seeing things that have not occurred.

· Generates compensatory attitudes such as crying, asking for forgiveness, making gifts, etc.

The feeling of loss is what makes jealousy accentuate. Spiritual theories know how to fight this emotion very well by making us aware that we have nothing. The seduction can also help. They are providing us with security to get ahead in case of losing a current relationship, or making us feel more confident if it helps us to make a relationship work well.

7. Emotional attachment or dependence

Managing emotions, such as attachment is vital to enjoying healthy relationships. The difficulty of controlling it lies in the shortcomings of the subject who suffers, often difficult to solve. Since the fact that a person understands, that depends on another to be happy in a clear sign of low esteem. That's why your first move ought to be to work on improving your self-esteem to learn to value yourself. Appreciating the richness of his life even when alone.

You live with many fears and frustrations thinking about how tragic life would be without the other.

· You feel that the other person is important, but you are not.

· Submission without concessions to what the other thinks or wants.

· It generates love obsessions difficult to bear and accused in tears.

· Feelings of abandonment and excessive fear to be left or set aside.

· Shyness and fear of losing the validation of the other.

· Loses consciousness and independence over one's abilities and talents.

· The constant search for others to meet their expectations also met the other way around. Feeling the responsibility to solve the problems of others.

· Feeling that life has no meaning if something is not given to others.

8. Anxiety or anguish

Emotional intelligence understands anguish as an emotion that defends us from situations that our mind perceives as dangerous. That is to say, all those that it is difficult to face. Materializing more frequently as anxiety. Being this useful to charge us with energy to face our challenges, but very harmful to health if it keeps us permanently in tension. Their characteristics are:

· Feelings of restlessness and fear, waiting for something bad to happen.

· It limits our ability to enjoy positive emotions, such as joy or love.

· It feeds doubt and perpetuates it. Continually asking ourselves what to do, what to say, or what choices to make.

· It causes us to escape or postpone situations that we should face.

· The tendency to calm this emotion with food, overwork, drugs, or medication.

9. Guilt

Feelings of guilt may be circumstantial or dragged throughout life. Feeling guilty at a specific moment when we see that we have made a mistake is healthy and normal. It's like a stop sign that tells us that this is not our way forward. However, we must manage and have this emotion well controlled when it is conditioning us negatively. That is when it causes us to act in a way that does not favor our interests; sometimes without realizing it.

· Arabia and prevents enjoy the present moment.

· Feel permanent debt to something or someone.

· It torments, and these doubts can be provoked by others to manipulate us.

· We feel that we are doing what we should.

· It generates that the one who blames himself also demands much from others, being able to generate states of dissatisfaction.

· The tendency to make accusations.

· Criticism and doubt towards the actions that have been undertaken.

Torment for decisions or past experiences. Being able to embitter the present and avoiding that you can turn the page. Which, in turn, coerces the freedom of current action because of fear?

CHAPTER 8 - ELIMINATING ANXIETY, STRESS AND FEAR

Once anxiety and stress take over your life, there ends up being a host of other problems including depression, headaches, insomnia, lack of appetite, and more. The most important thing to note is that for many, taking action might seem like the most difficult step, but it is through action that we can even hope to get rid of any amount of anxiety or stress. Let's look at ways you can deal with each of the two issues.

Working with Anxiety

Typically, anxiety is a situation that focuses on future affairs. Which is why you should make sure that every time you notice your mind wondering about the future, you bring yourself back to the present. The best way to go about that is to ask yourself the questions below:

- What is happening right now?
- What was your focus before anxiety decided to interrupt you?
- Is there something I should be worried about right now?
- Am I safe right now?

When you have answered the above questions, you can tell yourself that you will come back to them again at another point in the day so that you can dedicate time to think about yourself. Essentially, you are telling your mind not to interrupt your day and that you will be able to asses whatever is causing you anxiety at a particular point.

Meditate

Take 10 to 15 minutes every day to simply sit down somewhere you won't be interrupted and meditate. Calming yourself down might not be easy at first, but make sure that you practice every day until you are able to get it right. Here is a simple breathing exercise that you can follow:

- Find a place where you won't be interrupted for the next 10 to 15 minutes. You can either choose to sit or lie down on a comfortable surface.
- Once you have found a comfortable position, close your and eyes and take a few deep breaths.
- Once you have done that, bring your breathing back to normal.

- As you are breathing normally, bring your attention to your breathing.
- Now take a deep breath and as you do so, count to 5. Now hold your breath in and count to 3. Release your breath and let it last longer than the count of 5.
- Once again, bring your breathing back to normal. As you are breathing, you will notice that your mind might fill up with certain thoughts, ideas, or memories. They could be positive or negative. Regardless, do not ignore the thoughts. Make a mental note every time thoughts appear in your head and move on. If you are finding it difficult to move on from a thought, give it time to exit your mind.
- Continue breathing in this manner for the next 10 to 15 minutes. You can continue breathing longer if you like.
- Once you are done, take a few deep breaths again and bring your attention back to your surroundings. Notice the ground beneath your feet or the surface on which you are lying down. Notice the scents around you and the feel of the air on your body. Once you have grounded your mind in your surroundings, open your eyes.

Rethink Your Emotions

Try and acknowledge what you are feeling and relabel those feelings. For example, every time you get a panic attack, do not react to it. Instead, accept the fact that you are getting a panic attack and try your best to calm down. Then, remind yourself that this is temporary and that there is nothing for you to be worried about.

Be Realistic

Anxiety often makes you think about all the negative things that could happen to you. For example, if you are heading to an interview, then your anxiety might make you think that you are probably going to do terribly in the interview. But every time that happens, bring your attention to a realistic scenario. Think to yourself:

I have prepared myself for this. There are going to be challenges but I am going to do my best, regardless of the outcome.

By simply changing your thought structure, you are preventing your anxiety from taking control and your rational mind to drive your thoughts.

Slow Things Down

When anxiety attacks you, you are probably going to feel that your mind is zooming like a race car. Try focusing on your environment and then use lists to calm your mind. Look around you and make a note of three things that you can see. Then, focus on your hearing and note down three things that you can hear. You can even focus on an object in the environment and then note down three things about it. When you force yourself to focus on your environment, you are taking your attention away from your anxiety and focusing it on your surroundings.

Commit to an Act

If you start to feel the first signs of anxiety, then do something to distract yourself. Go ahead and make yourself some coffee. Take a walk outside. Engage in a conversation with someone. In fact, even doing some stretching exercises will suffice. The idea is to not allow anxiety to take over and ground yourself in the moment.

Maintain Good Posture

When we feel anxious, we are conscious of ourselves. We feel vulnerable and to protect ourselves from that vulnerability, we bring our shoulders together and hunch down. By simply walking or sitting with good posture, you are tricking your brain into thinking that everything is alright.

Avoid Sugar

According to researchers, sugar is harmful to your mental health (Lindberg, 2018). When you are hit with anxiety, you might feel a sudden craving for sugar. The problem with sugar itself is that your body releases insulin to deal with the excess glucose in the body. This makes the body work much harder than before to get back to a normal state. When you are feeling anxious, the last thing you want to do is overwork your body because that would mean you are going to experience highs and lows more frequently. This state of instability is harmful to your anxiety, as you are already experiencing highs and lows because of it.

Organize Yourself

Try not to get stuck in a rut when you are completing small tasks. People with anxiety always seek to get things under control. When you cannot accomplish even a simple task as finding your car keys, then your anxiety may shoot through the roof for the most trivial of reasons. Try this little hack to organize yourself:

- Choose a place to store your important stuff like car keys, wallet, and cards.
- Choose another place to store spare change and emergency cash.
- Finally, pick a place to keep important documents such as your passport or marriage documents so that you always know where to go when you need them.

Depending on how many items you have with you, you can choose multiple places to store them. The next thing you want to do is make a note of these places. Finally, make sure that you are putting your things in their designated spot.

By organizing things, you are avoiding a state of panic. You are preventing anxiety from taking control at the worst possible moment (for example, in the morning when you are about to head to work). Additionally, by putting things where they belong, you are bringing order into your life. A sense of order gives you control and that control, in turn, makes you feel powerful.

Challenge Negativity

Do not let negativity get free reign. Whenever you feel negative thoughts swimming through your mind, challenge them. Follow these steps to make sure that you get the upper hand over your negative thoughts:

Begin recording your thoughts whenever you get anxious.

Now explain what you feel when these thoughts enter your mind.

For example, you might be getting anxious about taking the subway because you think that people judge you. If fear is the emotion that comes to mind during this situation, then note down the word fear right next to your recorded event.

Next, use facts and rational thought to objectively question and analyze your anxiety.

In the above example, ask yourself if there truly is a reason for you to be worried about others' opinions? Besides, know that others might be going through the same emotions, even though they are not displaying it outwardly. Think about the fact that it does not matter what others think unless they are people you know. Think about the times that your family or friends enjoyed spending time with you, revealing the fact that you are loved by the people who care about you the most.

Coming up with rational thoughts for your anxiety can be rather challenging. But focus on your reality, your surroundings, the people in your life, and the knowledge that you have. If you truly wish to, go ahead and research a topic so you are more knowledgeable about it.

Working with Stress

The most important thing to focus on when you are stressed is the factor causing your stress. Once you can identify the source, you can take steps to prevent stress from overwhelming your life. Additionally, you need to be able to identify the fact that you are feeling stress. Most people ignore certain symptoms, believing that they are caused by other factors.

Identifying Stress

Know that there is a difference between just feeling tired or ill and experiencing stress. One way to identify stress is by looking out for other symptoms such as feeling extremely tired and lethargic, headaches or migraines, tense muscles, and constant worry. In such cases, you are not merely tired or ill, you are genuinely affected by stress.

Group Your Stress

Next, look at the causes of the stress and group them into one of three categories:

1. You are able to deal with the cause by using logical solutions
2. The situation will get better over time
3. There is nothing you can do about the cause of your stress

If you can do something about your stress, then create a practical plan to deal with the problem. However, if the cause of your stress falls into category 2 or 3, then try not to worry too much about those kinds of stress. They are beyond your control.

Recognize Your Responsibilities

Make a review of your work and ask yourself the following questions:

- How many responsibilities have you taken on your plate?
- Can you ask for someone's help to deal with some of the work you have to do?
- Are you taking free time for yourself?
- Can you organize your work so that you can deal with one task at a time?

Reduce the Intake of Addictive Substances

If you have been consuming alcohol or resorting to smoking and drugs, then try and cut them from your life. In the case of drugs, avoid them completely and for smoking and alcohol, see if you can reduce your intake to small levels of consumption.

Workout or Exercise

If you can hit the gym or take part in physical activity, then make sure that you take advantage of that. In fact, simply spending time outdoors has a positive effect on your health and mind (Heart.org, 2018). Try and see if you can incorporate some light exercises into your routine.

Take Some Time Off Work

If you feel that stress overwhelms your life, then there is no harm from taking some time out for yourself. A little break improves your productivity at work and allows you to examine the problem from a different perspective. Convince yourself that it is okay to take care of yourself, as you might be stuck in a mental loop where you might think that being busier is good for you when in reality, it is not.

Practice Mindfulness

Through mindfulness, people can examine their thoughts and feelings to better cope with bad situations in their life. One of the best ways to incorporate mindfulness is by practicing meditation frequently.

Avoid Punishing Yourself

You must have seen quotes about people pushing themselves to the edge in order to accomplish something. The thing is, they are neglecting other plans; one where they are relaxing on a beautiful beach with a martini in hand.

Try putting your life into perspective and check to see if you are managing your time well between your work life and your personal life. See if you have been spending time with the people you care about.

Additionally, if you feel that your mind has been too critical on yourself, then try and analyze each critical thought. Ask yourself if your mind is truly justified in forming these thoughts. Think of the times that you had reacted too critically towards yourself. Perhaps by repeatedly being harsh on yourself, your emotional subconscious has picked up on your reactions and is now creating similar thoughts.

What you need to do is train your emotional subconscious to motivate you. The task might not be simple if you have been facing critical thoughts for some time, but you know what they say about practice and perfection. Every day, create a list of three things that are good qualities about yourself. Memorize these qualities. Every time you receive a negative thought during the rest of the day, repeat the positive traits you had memorized. The next day, pick three new positive traits and repeat the exercise. Through this simple exercise, not only are you training your emotional subconscious to examine you from a more positive light, but you are also showing yourself that there are so many things positive about you.

Get Good Sleep

Do not sacrifice a good night's sleep to complete the project you have been working on. Try and organize your day so that you can perform with maximum efficiency without having to allow your work to interrupt your sleep. If are indeed faced with a project that looks like it is not going to let you catch some z's, then make up for your lost sleep the next day or the day after that. However, do not remain sleep deprived for more than a day or two at most (in fact, even two days of little sleep are harmful, but if you really have to, then make sure you have done everything by the second day).

Fear

Whenever we try something new, we experience anxiety. We are afraid of the unknown. This is why we like to maintain our daily routine and stay within our comfort zones. From our brain's point of view, this makes perfect sense. If our current habits allow us to be safe and avoid any potential threat to our survival (or the survival of our ego) why bother changing them? This explains why we often keep the same routine, or have the same thoughts over and over. It is also why we may experience a lot of internal resistance when trying to change ourselves.

Thus, when we try to move beyond our comfort zones, we experience fear and distress. Now, do we want to stay in the same place most of our lives and avoid taking any risks, or do we want to pursue our dreams and see what we are truly capable of becoming? We have to remember, most of our fears are a threat only to our ego, not to our survival. Generally, they aren't physical threats, but imaginary ones. If we play it safe we risk missing out on life, and we may regret it later.

Below are common fears you may experience:

Fear of rejection: You're afraid of being rejected. This may be physical rejection from a specific group, but it is generally more subtle. For instance, you may be afraid of:

•Making a comment people could disapprove of

•Asking someone out and being turned down, or

•Sharing your work and being criticized for it.

Fear of failure: You're afraid of failing. This usually comes from the deepest fear of not being good enough, i.e. you are afraid of being ridiculed and believe that failure will erode your self-esteem.

Fear of loss: Human beings have an aversion to loss, which is why we are often more motivated to prevent a loss than to secure a gain.

Fear of disturbing: You're afraid of disturbing people. Perhaps due to the belief you're not important enough. As a result, you may feel reluctant to affirm yourself for fear of appearing selfish.

Fear of success: You're afraid of success. You may worry you won't be able to sustain it with all the added pressure on your shoulders.

How to use fear to grow

The fear of doing something new is often a sign you should go ahead and do it anyway. This indicates a great opportunity for personal growth. Fear, as with any other emotion, only exists in your mind. This is why we often realize what a fool we've been after we've completed something we were initially wary of starting.

People who end up reaching their wildest goals often do so because they are willing to leave their comfort zone. Over time, they learn to be comfortable with the uncomfortable. Picture one thing you were once afraid to do, that is now no big deal for you. For instance, I bet you were scared the first time you drove, or on your first day at work. Now, didn't you get used to it?

The truth is, people have the formidable ability to learn. The key is to grow accustomed to experiencing discomfort once in a while. By not facing your fears on a regular basis, you will greatly limit your potential for development. Staying inside your comfort zone can also erode your sense of self-esteem as, in the back of your mind, you know you're not doing what you're supposed to do.

There is a law in nature: things either grow or die. The same goes for humans beings. When humans don't move beyond their comfort zone, they start dying inside. Don't let that happen to you. As Benjamin Franklin said, "Some people die at twenty-five and aren't buried until seventy-five." Make sure 'some people' doesn't include you!

Taking action

The first step to move out of your comfort zone is to realize even the most successful people on earth feel fear. Courage is not the absence of fear, it is taking action despite the fear. Courage is realizing fear is not going to go away and doing what you want to do anyway. Without fear, there is no courage. As you face fear on a regular basis, you cultivate courage and turn it into a habit.

You don't need to avoid fear or numb yourself to it before you can take action. Instead, you must accept the fact that fear won't go away and get used to it. Then, you must decide to take action.

Exercise - Move out of your comfort zone

To start moving out of your comfort zone, you can ask yourself, "What is the one thing I should be doing, but fear has made me procrastinate over?" Once you do that one thing, you'll likely experience a sense of pride and of being alive. This is a sign you're on the right track. See it as the reward your brain gives you for moving beyond your comfort zone.

CHAPTER 9 - THE RELATIONSHIP BETWEEN EMOTIONAL INTELLIGENCE AND LEADERSHIP

Being a leader is a position which commands huge responsibility. All eyes are constantly on you. When a challenge or conflict arises, you're the one people turn to for solutions and answers. It is a big responsibility to oversee and manage a team of people, and the pressure to perform, to ensure that things are always running smoothly, rests on your shoulders.

No team, project or organization can succeed without good leadership leading the way which is why emotional intelligence is so important. When you've got so much on your plate to deal with, you're bound to go through all sorts of emotions. If you don't learn to manage and control those emotions, they're going to overwhelm you easily. Being a leader, and being an effective leader, are two very different things. The latter is the one that is destined for success.

Managing a company alone is overwhelming, but being an effective leader to a team of people who are the backbone of your company is an even more overwhelming task. You must be an effective leader if you're going to bring out the best in the people that you work with. A leader needs to constantly evaluate their leadership method to see if their approaches are working as well as they should.

Part of being an effective manager is knowing the strengths and weaknesses of your team members, and what each person brings to the table. This part can be achieved through the social skills, motivation and empathy part of the emotional intelligence core principles. An effective leader will never turn a blind eye to conflict and will do everything in their power to address the conflict as soon as it happens. To do this, you need to effectively tune into the emotions of the people who are involved in the conflict. Empathize with them, see where they're coming from. During conflict is when emotions tend to run high, and if you're not able to properly manage your own emotions, you won't be able to manage the emotions of others.

How to become an effective and aware leader

An effective leader is one that is not afraid of a challenge. Effective leadership is also not about bossing people around. It isn't just about telling them what to do. Effective leadership is about bringing out all the best qualities in all the people you work it, to get a team of people working together like a well-oiled machine. An effective leader breeds success. Effective leaders share in the responsibility and the workload of the team. They're not afraid to get down and dirty with the team, being one with the rest of them and taking on jobs that everyone else is doing.

As an effective leader, the responsibility also lies with you to let your team know you're always there for them no matter what. You need to let your people know that they matter to you. You need to nurture them, encourage them to grow in their way, empathize and be compassionate when you see that they are struggling. Emotional intelligence is your secret weapon to bringing out the best in your employees because it can help you connect with them in ways you couldn't imagine. This isn't just another boss-employee relationship. To be considered an effective and successful leader, you need to go the extra mile and look beyond that.

How do you use emotional intelligence to foster effective leadership and become more aware? By employing the following techniques:

•**Let Your Team Know They Matter** - People are emotional creatures. As a leader, if you want to be successful and effective, it is your job to listen to everyone's, and what they have to say. Make it your policy to encourage everyone to approach you and give them a chance to express themselves. Let them know they can come and talk to you about how they feel without judgment. Your job is to be encouraging, to empathize with them and make them feel supported. To make them feel like they matter.

•**Be Someone Who's Trustworthy** - You need to cultivate an environment of trust at all times when you are with their team. When a team can trust each other, they work much better together. When they know without a doubt, they can put their full trust in their leader to always have their best interest at heart, that makes for a happier, more positive team all around.

•**Forging Strong Connections** - Use the self-awareness and social skills aspect of emotional intelligence to help you foster stronger connections between you and the people you manage. Don't just connect for the sake of doing so, but build a connection that is meaningful, that shows the team members you genuinely care about them and their welfare. Reach out to them on a regular basis, congratulate them when they successfully meet their targets. Catch up with them regularly and talk about common interests. Ask them about their families, their hobbies, their passion. Build a relationship outside of just work matters.

•**Show Empathy** - There's a reason why this is one of the core principles of emotional intelligence. The people in your team have emotions and feelings, put yourself in their shoes and try to imagine what they would be feeling. This makes it much easier for you to see things from their perspective, to understand where they're coming from and why they're feeling the way that they do. An effective leader is one who can practice empathy and compassion with sincerity.

•**Listen Attentively** - When having a one-on-one conversation with a member of your team, listen to their voice inflections and the tone of their voice. Pay attention to the words they use, the points they emphasize on. Listen to the way they sound when they talk about how they feel. Self-awareness is what you need in this case. Practicing self-awareness (another EQ core principle) and listening attentively will help you connect with your people, and be empathetic towards them. It will help you be compassionate, understanding and nurturing in all the ways that they need.

•**Be Mutually Respectful** - Respect and encourage respect among every single person in the organization and team, because everyone has a role to play and their role contributes to the overall success. The most effective type of leaders are ones that provide a work environment where employees help each other and value the contributions that each makes. This can only be achieved by master emotional intelligence because without the crucial self-awareness, motivational and social skills needed, you're going to find it very hard to manage yourself and everyone else.

•**Take Time to Reflect On Your Feelings** - Leaders are sometimes so busy looking after everyone else that they forget to check in with themselves and their feelings. Part of being an effective leader with high levels of emotional intelligence is about being able to check in with yourself now and then. What have your feelings been lately? Reflect on them for several moments. This helps to avoid you falling out of touch with yourself and everyone else around you. Leaders have a lot on their plate, and they can be so busy trying to manage everything else that they forget stopping to take care of themselves is something they need to do.

•**Taking Breaks When You Need It** - Leaders are always expected to bring their A-game and be switched on all the time. It is easy to forget that leaders are people too, with feelings and emotions. They too, like everyone else, can burn out if they fail to take care of themselves. They too can be easily drained by having to manage all sorts of emotions. The emotionally intelligent thing to do is to stop and take breaks whenever you need them. It is perfectly okay to take some time to recharge your batteries. In fact, you should make it a point to do this to keep you drowning in your own emotions. Being a leader is challenging, and it can take a toll on you emotionally, mentally and physically. Whenever you think you need a break to recharge, take it and don't feel guilty about doing so.

As a leader with huge amounts of responsibility on your shoulders, you need emotional intelligence to help you sort through your feelings in healthy ways. Emotional intelligence teaches you how to regulate your impulses, so you don't act out emotionally and in the heat of the moment, because that's not what an effective leader does. That's how your people end up losing trust in you if you appear to be a leader who is unpredictable and acts out emotionally. EQ does make a big difference in the level of success you achieve because it trains you to focus on what matters. It teaches you to remain calm, focused and in control in the moments when you need it most. More importantly, it teaches you how to get a handle on the negative emotions that could threaten to disrupt your success. It teaches you to be mindful and to be attuned to the way that you're feeling at crucial moments. That is how emotional intelligence helps you become a more effective and aware leader.

CHAPTER 10 - THE IMPORTANCE OF EMPATHY

The role of empathy in emotional intelligence cannot be overstated. In fact, empathy is often taken as an indicator of emotional intelligence. This is perhaps because empathy is a quality that many people understand, or at least believe that they do, and it can, therefore, be used as a symbol of what makes emotional intelligence, and by extension, human beings, exceptional. In this regard, empathy is a sort of mascot for emotional intelligence. But as the reader has already seen, empathy is a term that is often misused or misunderstood.

Most people recognize the utility of feeling compassion for others and the importance of tolerance. Compassion is part of recognizing someone else as being a human being with much the same feelings, pains, and joys that we ourselves experience. Tolerance perhaps comes with age and experience, and it involves recognizing that others are different from us and that these differences are okay. But this feeling of deep compassion and tolerance, even if it has a strong emotional component, is not precisely empathy.

On the other end of the spectrum, some people have the image of a person who feels too deeply. This person is so weighted down with emotion and the deep and subjective experience of it that they are practically incapable of functioning. This person has empathy (true empathy, as will be defined shortly), but this trait is so dysfunctional for them that this is as much a curse as it is a blessing. This is the image of the empath, the person who is able to experience the emotions of others uncontrollably. Though this is empathy, this is not exactly the type of trait that we are exploring here in our examination of emotional intelligence.

Indeed, empathy, when used properly, is a trait that confers an enormous benefit to the person that wields it. As the saying goes, people may not remember what you have said to them, but they will remember how you made them feel. As the empath is able to experience the subjective emotional states of others, they are able to interact with these others with a deep emotional connection. This is key to empathy as a component of emotional intelligence. This is a trait or skill that works in conjunction with other skills to guide behavior and in so doing to facilitate human interaction.

Defining Empathy

The first step, therefore, becomes one of defining what precisely empathy is. In every science, it is important to begin by defining terms so that everyone knows just what precisely is being dealt with. This is just as true in social science as it is in the study of machine learning and artificial intelligence where computer scientists program the AI agent with data definitions. As empathy is a crucial component of EI, it is a data definition that you will have to understand well if you plan to infuse your life with emotional intelligence. As you have seen, the benefits of doing so are many.

Empathy is the capacity to feel the subjective emotions or experiences of others. A person that has empathy would not only be perceptive of when another feels sadness, or feel compassion for them in their particular emotional state, but they would actually share that state. An empathic person would feel sadness when the other feels sadness. As was touched on earlier, this is an ability that can be very moving for the person experiencing it, and therefore could have both positive and negative consequences depending on what the result of this empathetic experience is.

The key with empathy, to reiterate, is that it is used with other components of emotional intelligence like self-awareness, self-regulation, and motivation. Empathy on its own (like self-awareness, for example) can sometimes be problematic. Empathy is also occasionally defined as consisting of three components of its own. These are accuracy, compassion, and interactions. The purpose of this type of definition is to point out that a key to true empathy is, the empathetic individual is accurate in their emotional awareness and the awareness is somehow demonstrated in an interaction.

The Difference Between Empathy And Sympathy

The issue that always arises with empathy is how to distinguish it from sympathy. Earlier, we showed how an individual could feel compassion and tolerance for others. We noted that this is an important component of empathy, but that technically, empathy goes far beyond this particular experience. In fact, compassion and tolerance are hallmarks of sympathy. A sympathetic person feels compassion for others, and they show this with a sympathetic look or comforting words.

An empathetic person has compassion and is receptive enough of the other person's experiences and feelings to feel tolerance, but they are able to share that person's feelings and experiences by actually experiencing them themselves. Clearly, one individual cannot in actuality literally experience the subjective experiences of another, but the empathetic person feels so deeply that it is as if they have experienced the same things that the other has. It might be convenient to think about experiences and feelings as being subjective states of the brain modulated by brain chemistry, and the person with empathy is able to mirror the subjective state that the other experiences as dictated by their brain chemistry.

An important aspect of empathy to recall is that empathy, unlike sympathy, is not something that is shown but had. Certainly, human beings have ways of showing that they are making an emotional connection with someone else, that they feel compassion for them, but this is not the same as sharing the subjective experiences that someone else is living through. Empathy is something that is experienced rather than something that an individual merely understands or feels compassion for. Again, the image of the empath comes to mind. But in the context of emotional intelligence, empathy becomes a step in forming an emotional connection with other people.

How To Practice Empathy

One of the things that make emotional intelligence such an exciting field to study and read about is that it is not something static as traditional cognitive reasoning is often thought to be. Emotional intelligence abilities can be traits that one inherits, and one demonstrates from childhood, or they can be skills that one acquires and improves over time. This is true of empathy just as much as it is true of the other components of EI. Empathy skills can be improved by practicing them. Indeed, even people with minimal empathic skills can acquire them and cause them to grow with the right training.

So how does one go about practicing empathy? Practicing empathy generally requires that you channel some of the other components of emotional intelligence, even if empathy is a thing distinct and powerful. First of all, you must be motivated to have empathy in order to go about practicing. Understand that empathy can improve your ability to connect with others. Second, you must practice being perceptive of the emotions of others. Some people are totally insensitive of the feelings of others. Most human beings are able to recognize emotion. You need to focus on recognizing the emotion of others and caring about it.

Another important step in having empathy is talking about it. This may seem strange, but studies have shown that emotional sensitivity improves when people talk about it. For some people, this may include some self-talk. For example, if one of your co-workers appears upset, you may say to yourself: "Susan appears upset. Why? I wonder what is going on with her." This talking about feeling empathy will lead to you caring about the feelings of others in ways you perhaps did not before.

Finally, the last and most important part of practicing empathy is actually feeling the emotions and experiences of others. Some experience this naturally while to others, this may be a completely foreign concept. As you go through the steps of practicing empathy, you may find that this subjective experience of sharing another's feelings becomes easier and more natural. The steps are summarized here:

- Be motivated to have empathy for others
- Be perceptive of the feelings of others and not just your own
- Feel compassion for others (sympathy)
- Talk about the feelings of others (even if it is just to yourself)
- Practice caring about the feelings of others rather than just recognizing them

CHAPTER 11 - TIPS AND EXERCISES FOR SLEEP

Calming yourself can be particularly difficult if you struggle with relaxation. However, learning to relax and sleep can help your emotional intelligence—self-care is an incredibly important part of your emotional intelligence because if you do not care for yourself, you are in no position to care for anyone else either. If you are exhausted, your mind is in no state to take care of others or manage your own emotions. You need your rest to be an effective person and a respected member of society. This chapter will provide you with four tips and exercises to help you relax and better your quality of sleep.

Keep a Sleep Schedule and Routine

It can be hard to sleep when your circadian rhythm is all out of whack. You need your rhythm in order to cue your body when it is time to sleep and wake. It keeps you healthy and helps you to regulate your hormones. Even on weekends or vacations, keeping your sleep schedule consistent can do wonders for the quality of your sleep.

Before you sleep, however, you need to have some sort of routine you follow that triggers your body that it is time to get ready for bed. Bedtime routines are not just for children—they can actually be fantastic for adults as well. When you have a set schedule and routine, your body will naturally begin to wind down around the same time every day. Your body naturally wants to gravitate toward a specific schedule. You may notice that you are hungry around the same time every day, want your coffee at the same time every day, get tired at the same time every day, and more. This is because your body regulates itself. Your body naturally wants to adhere to a schedule that it can predict because it has hormones that run on a cycle.

If you want to set up a sleep routine, keep it relaxed. Maybe take a shower and lie down in bed with a book and a cup of warm, caffeine-free tea. Drink your tea and read your book for an hour, but make sure it is a paper book as opposed to something digital—the light from your screen will interfere with the sleeping hormones your body naturally produces. After you read for an hour, brush your teeth and lay down in bed. Make sure you are getting to bed at the same time every night, and make sure phones and lights are off. Good sleep hygiene means keeping the screens out of the bedroom, no matter how tempting it may be to keep them present.

Exercise Daily

When you exercise daily, you are able to keep your body healthy and regulated. It produces hormones that will keep your body on schedule, happy, and healthy. It is recommended that people get at least 150 minutes of exercise a week in order to stay healthy and keep your body functioning regularly.

When you exercise regularly, you are able to lessen anxiety, insomnia, and depression, and it keeps the body's circadian rhythm regular. Ultimately, keeping your body healthy seems to be one of the most effective ways to keep your sleep regular as well. Your body will thank you if you go for that after-dinner walk every day.

Your exercise can be anything. You could go to the gym and lift weights, swim, walk your dog several times a week, or even just buy a little desk cycle and pedal under your desk as you work. Anything is okay so long as you are getting the blood pumping regularly. It will keep your blood pressure healthy and alleviate the stress that might otherwise keep you awake at night.

Breathing Exercise

When you are lying in bed and struggling to sleep, try this breathing exercise.

You should start with your eyes closed. Pay attention to your breathing, but do not alter it. Focus as you inhale the air, feeling it go through your airway and all the way to your lungs. Imagine seeing the air as it spreads to your lungs, filling out all of the little alveoli and finally flooding into your blood. Exhale the air. Feel how your body changes as you do so.

Notice how your diaphragm and stomach rise and fall, expanding with your inhalations and deflating as you exhale. Look for any other areas that seem to feel tense. Take another deep breath, and as you do so, identify anywhere that is tense. Imagine the tenseness is all bundled into your breath, and exhale. As you exhale, feel the tenseness leave as well. Keep yourself entirely relaxed as you continue. Inhale slowly and deeply, feeling the air fill out your lungs, and imagine your worries and stresses melding with the breath. As you exhale, imagine those worries leaving with the breath.

You may notice your mind wander, and that is okay. Gently redirect your mind back to your inhalation and exhalation, and focus on the rhythm, the way your body changes, and how relaxed you are beginning to feel. As you do this, you may find yourself relaxing enough to fall asleep altogether.

Guided Imagery

Guided imagery is essentially daydreaming, but you do so in order to relieve your stress and worries. When you do this, you are trying to relax enough so you can finally fall asleep.

Start by getting comfortable. All lights should be out and you should be ready to sleep. Once you are comfortable, close your eyes. Take a few deep, calming breaths and let go of any tenseness in your body. Think of a place that brings you calmness. It could be the place where you met your significant other, a trip you took by yourself, a beautiful sunset, church, your backyard, or anywhere. It does not matter where the place is, so long as it brings you calmness. Then, carry out some sort of story or activity at that location. Visualize it as clearly as you can, with all of the details, and keep it meticulous. You want to notice every single detail. For the purpose of an example, I will use a beach at sunset.

Imagine the beach. The sky is a beautiful gradient from the warmest orange you could ever imagine, to pink, to lavender, to blue, all the way to darkness on the other horizon. The ocean laps calmly over the sand. Imagine the sound of the water gently caressing the shore and think of how relaxing it is.

Imagine yourself walking along the sand, feeling it crunch under your feet and the waves that just barely tickle the bottom of your feet. As you walk, you are able to see stars starting to appear in the sky, one by one. You notice as they appear, with the sky quickly growing darker than you expected. Soon, all that is left in the sky are the stars, and the gentle sounds of the water washing up onshore.

Any time you find yourself distracted, just slowly and calmly redirect yourself back to the story. Let yourself get lost in the story or the scene, really enjoying it. It does take practice to be able to truly lose yourself in this manner so do not feel discouraged if you feel as though you have struggled. The more you practice, the better you will get.

CHAPTER 12 - APPLYING EMOTIONAL INTELLIGENCE IN YOUR LIFE

How well do you resolve conflict? Are you always creating conflict? How are you at anger management? How well do you deal with adversity?

Are you quick to give criticism? How well do you take it? Are you an effective problem solver? Can you motivate yourself? How do you respond to the feelings and emotions of others?

These questions get to the heart of Emotional Intelligence. Answering them honestly, you will start to get to the meat of your EI muscle, and start to develop it. Other questions are:

•How comfortable, if at all, are you in exchanging your thoughts and feelings with your intimate partner, or with your family?

•Can you build cooperative relationships, or are most of your relationships destructive?

•How do you deal with difficult people; do you blame them for being difficult; or are you self-aware enough to realize that it is your own in-effectiveness in dealing with others that makes them difficult?

•Do you have a strong group of supportive people around you?

•Do you attract adversarial relationships?

•Do you feel like the victim, more often than not?

These everyday barometers indicate whether or not you are applying your Emotional Intelligence in your life. They give you an idea of how effectively you are using your emotions, feelings, moods, and those of others as a source of information to help you navigate through life more effectively.

Evidence suggests that applying your Emotional Intelligence will enhance all aspects of your life significantly. Consider briefly the following five factors that make up Emotional Intelligence:

•Self-Awareness, or your ability to accurately process information about yourself

•Mood Management, or your ability to manage your emotions, rid yourself of bad moods and create positive ones

•Self-Motivation, or your ability to persist, overcome frustration, engage in necessary yet boring tasks, initiate productive actions and to cut out counterproductive ones

•Interpersonal expertise, or your ability to give and take criticism, work out conflict, build consensus, and develop cooperative relationships

•Emotional mentoring, or your ability to respond effectively to the emotions and feelings of others, to help others to solve problems

Each of these factors has an impact on your life. They affect how you parent, how you navigate your relationships or marriage, and they have a significant impact on your work life. Given that we need to use our Emotional Intelligence to succeed in all these areas of our life, it is therefore critical that you develop and apply your Emotional Intelligence in your life.

It is especially important that you learn to apply Emotional Intelligence in your work life, but to neglect any of the other areas of your life would be detrimental. The first step to applying Emotional Intelligence in your own life involves recognizing the driving emotions in our lives.

The Importance Of Self-Awareness

When asked what the three emotions are that drive what you do every day, it is not surprising that the overwhelming majority of people list anxiety, frustration and fear. When we are anxious or frustrated, this can lead to low levels of productivity at work, and when we are fearful, this leads to tension and conflict on the home front. This is because many people do not have appropriate responses for these emotions, and cannot deal sufficiently and constructively with them.

This has a number of adverse effects, including:

•Weight Gain

•Smoking Far Too Much

•Alcohol and Drug Abuse

It is therefore imperative that you learn to control these emotions, or your response to them, so that you avoid going down the destructive path that is paved with proverbial good intentions.

The good news is this is something that you can learn. You can learn to apply your EI, even though you have never been formally taught how. What you need to do is to consider firstly your inner dialogue, the thoughts that you hold uppermost in your mind. This will influence how you feel and act.

Too many people are not even aware of the dialogue that they have with themselves. So unaware are they of the thoughts that are running through their minds that many of us end up using our own thoughts against us. An increase in self-awareness, particularly of your inner dialogue, can bring you to a point where your thoughts work for you and not against you.

You will start to notice whether you tend to blow things out of proportion, magnifying the significance of a situation. You will also notice if you have the habit of coloring your perceptions of others with negatives; or whether you engage in self-demeaning thoughts and statements.

Being aware of these habits will make you mindful to change them. This will take some time to get used to doing. So why not start right now! Taking even a few minutes a day to really listen to how you talk to yourself is an easy way to increase your awareness of how you talk to yourself and help you develop your EI and apply it!

Managing Your Moods Is Critical!

How many times have you been told to 'snap out of it?' When you're having a bad day, or feeling a little less than chipper, it is the last thing that you want to hear. However, the ability to manage your emotions is a skill that will serve you very well in your pursuit of happiness.

So, how do you 'snap out of it?'

The first step is to understand where your emotion comes from. Being aware of what is going on in your head is a good step to help you identify the root of your mood. What has happened in the recent while that changed your mood, or who 'happened' to you? Why do you feel the way you do about this person or event?

Answering these questions will help you manipulate your mood and replace your 'bad' mood with a 'good' one.

Motivating Yourself!

Self-Motivation is an art. It requires real work, more so than most endeavors that you will undertake in your life. The ability to persist, often in the face of great adversity can take real gumption. Forging your way, often frustratingly through the boring 'must do' tasks on your to do list can be overwhelming.

Are there any ways to make every action a productive one, and to counter unproductive ones, however?

Some actions will take natural priority on your list of things to do. Others however, will not rank highly, but they will be essential if you are to move forward with the task at hand. Think of administration and paperwork, when your primary business is giving helicopter rides. Or even cleaning the kitchen before you can bake that chocolate cake that you have been looking forward to baking all week.

You will need to dig deep within yourself to find the energy and drive for you to accomplish the mundane, so that you can go on and accomplish greater and better things. The old adage, do what you must so that you can do what you want to, rings very true here.

We have also all met those people, the ones with great work ethic, who care about quality and are committed to improving themselves, but who rarely get rewarded for their efforts. We have also met their co-worker, the one who is no more hardworking or qualified, but who gets recognition and is often promoted.

Some people just seem to have to work harder for rewards, and no matter how hard they try, they never get past begin. Nothing can be as disheartening as this. Being on the receiving end of this treatment does little to motivate you, especially in the context of a team.

You need to motivate yourself when this happens. You need to go on and get things done, to the best of your ability, regardless of how you feel inside.

Mastering Interpersonal Situations

Applying Emotional Intelligence in your life involves being able to take criticism. You also need to be able to give constructive criticism, without coming across as demeaning or condescending. This is a fine balancing act. You must be able to take it as good as you give it.

Another critical key is being able to work out conflict in an amicable way. This will help you to build consensus and to develop cooperative relationships that work in your personal and in your professional life.

Filtering Emotions

What is the benefit of honing all the above skills? Well, you will develop your ability to respond effectively to the emotions and feelings of others. You will become the go to person when other people need to solve problems.

Whether you need a little bit of brushing up, or you rank way below average and need to work on your EI, now is the best time to do that. There are a number of tests that you can take online that will give you an indication of where you rank in terms of your Emotional Intelligence. You will have seen also that there are a number of offline, real world evaluations that give you an even better idea of how strong you are emotionally!

You will be able to express yourself correctly, to the correct people. You will be able to shift your focus so that you can bring about more empowering emotions in yourself. You will be able to control your impulses and make wise decisions.

Being able to read people's emotional states, you will be able to engage authentically with them. This will allow you to adapt your behavior quickly and easily in any setting that you find yourself in. You will be able to articulate your understanding of other people's perspectives respectfully, so that they feel understood.

You will be able to avoid addictive or destructive behaviors, meaning you will not smoke, or drink too much. And you certainly will not engage in recreational drug use. You will be able to address conflict quickly, and with confidence.

You will be self-motivated, and you will not need deadlines from outside sources to get projects started. In a nutshell, you will be able to leverage social awareness to inspire others positively so that they are consistently authentic in the dealing with you and perform at their best.

So the next time someone's cologne is too strong, or you're tempted to say something 'private' that might be overheard by someone else, or a friend asks for your opinion on a new romantic partner of whom you disapprove, you can apply what you know about EI to any of these situations.

CHAPTER 13 - MYTHS ABOUT EMOTIONAL INTELLIGENCE

As is the case with a lot of things, there exist several misconceptions regarding emotional intelligence. Throughout the course of this book, you've probably been able to identify the misconceptions you have had about emotional intelligence yourself, and the accompanying truth of the matter. This chapter is dedicated to busting the many myths that a whole lot of people have when it comes to EQ. Some of the myths are laughable while others are downright ridiculous. Seeing that EQ deals with emotion, it is probably not too unexpected that there would be numerous feelings expressed on the same. Dive in to find out what is true about emotional intelligence and what isn't.

Myth: Emotional intelligence is a woman's area

Truth: Emotional intelligence is a skill that applies to both men and women.

For the longest time, the stereotype of women being more emotional than men has been perpetuated by various channels. It, therefore, follows that when most people hear of emotional intelligence they only think of women. This could not be further from the truth. First of all, the claim that women are the more emotional of the human species is not a claim that is supported by biology. When scientists set out to study this phenomenon, they found out that the populations observed were more likely to behave according to the expectations placed on them by their cultures rather than as dictated by nature. In other words, women might behave more emotionally since that is what society or culture dictates from them, while men might repress their emotions for the same reason.

Seeing that we are capable of emotion, regardless of gender, it follows that there is a need to understand and manage those emotions. Even if there was a parallel universe where males were virtually incapable of having emotions, they would still be required to deal with women who, clearly, have emotions. As such, emotional intelligence is a scale that these parallel universe males would require when interacting with the parallel universe women.

Myth: Emotional intelligence is the sole determinant for success in life.

Truth: There are many factors that determine whether you will be successful in life and EQ happens to be one of them.

Emotional intelligence opens a lot of doors for you in life. When you are able to read and relate well with people, you do not have as many obstacles when compared to someone who has low EQ. However, EQ is not the all-inclusive package for success. Success requires a combination of smarts, hard work, opportunity or chance, and sometimes even sheer luck. Being low in the EQ does not automatically qualify you for failure. In fact, there are some professions where people become highly successful just by relying on their IQ.

An engineer, for instance, might be required to have a very high IQ so that they can easily grasp concepts. The same engineer might be very low on the EQ front and still go on to become highly successful because their work calls for smarts over emotional intelligence. Sure, the engineer might struggle with personal relationships and will probably never hold a management position, but they will still be successful in their own right.

Myth: Emotional intelligence is about being nice.

Truth: Emotional intelligence is more than just being nice.

Over the years, nice has grown to be synonymous with being a pushover or a doormat. Whenever people hear that someone is nice, they start to imagine all manner of ways they can walk all over that person. Here's the thing: If you think of nice as the capacity to tolerate people's personalities and their idiosyncrasies, then yes, emotional intelligence is about being nice. However, if your definition of nice is being the person that says yes to every request and does not have a voice of their own, then you are way off from what emotional intelligence actually is. Emotional intelligence does not make you a yes-man. In fact, emotional intelligence equips you with all the skills that you need to be able to say no as many times as you need and to do so unapologetically.

Myth: You're either born with emotional intelligence or not.

Truth: You can learn to become more emotionally intelligent.

Emotional intelligence is not the same as height whereby you are either born tall or short and are thereafter doomed to never reaching the higher shelves or always being the brunt of height jokes. Sure, some people have a higher ability to grasp emotional intelligence. This might depend on how they are born, how they are raised, the experiences they have been through, and numerous other factors that they interact with as they become adults. However, most people are capable of being emotionally intelligent. Even psychopaths who are incapable of feeling emotions like the rest of us know how to mimic emotional intelligence. If you are a fully functional human being with a wide range of emotions then you are fully capable of being emotionally intelligent.

Myth: Everyone that knows how to charm people is emotionally intelligent.

Truth: Sometimes there is more than emotional intelligence behind the charm.

Some of the most charming people you know are also the most dangerous human beings that you'll ever cross paths with. Just because a person knows when and how to smile in your face does not mean that they are high in EQ. They might just be manipulative. Psychopaths, for instance, know how to blend in and play Mr. Sociable Guy role to perfection. While an emotionally intelligent person will make you feel relaxed and comfortable without invading your personal space, a psychopath that is trying to win your trust may be more forceful, persistent and full-on in a manner that might be uncomfortable. A trick you can use to determine whether you are dealing with high EQ or psychopathy is by trusting your gut feeling, watching whether someone's actions match their words and noticing how you feel after every interaction. If you are leaving conversations feeling drained and unsure, you might be dealing with an energy vampire in the form of a psychopath rather than an emotionally intelligent person.

Myth: Introverts are not usually emotionally intelligent.

Truth: Introverts can be as emotionally intelligent as anyone else.

Introverts are known (or at least stereotyped) to be these shy and socially awkward people who have little to zero chance of ever being good at normal social interactions. While there may be some truth to it, this is not exactly the textbook definition of an introvert. An introvert is simply someone who prefers to look into themselves rather than turning to their external world for stimulation. An introvert is content in their own company and will often prefer to be silent rather than to talk. An introvert's worst nightmare is the extrovert, especially the kind of extrovert who does not have any emotional intelligence. Now, just because a person prefers to be silent does not mean that they are low in emotional intelligence. In fact, the fact that introverts are inward-looking means that they probably already have the self-awareness bit of EQ figured out. However, because introverts tend to be so absorbed in their worlds (in the most unselfish way possible) it means that they have to work a little harder at drawing themselves out into their external environment.

Seeing that introversion is a personality type, and personalities are not known scientifically to be dynamic, an introvert will often face the uphill task of opening up their world to other people. For instance, you cannot be empathetic to the suffering of others unless you are aware of this suffering. To become aware of this suffering, you must at least speak with this person so that they can tell you that yes indeed they are having a bad day. This can be almost too much to ask from an introvert.

The good news is that emotional intelligence can be learned since it is a skill like any other. An introvert is able to pick up the cues that they need to incorporate to be emotionally intelligent just like all other personality types. In fact, there are introverts out there who are highly emotionally intelligent. They know how to carry themselves when they are in a group of people. They understand that certain circumstances call for them to leave the security of their shells. Once they are back home, they quietly retreat to the safety of their shell until further circumstances require them to come out.

Myth: Emotional intelligence is only important for people in leadership roles or in particular professions.

Truth: Emotional intelligence makes your life easier regardless of who you are.

When you are in a leadership position, your lack of emotional intelligence will be more apparent and detrimental compared to a lack of emotional intelligence in the people that you lead or any other person. It has been said that with great power comes great responsibility and this could not be truer when it comes to emotional intelligence. When you serve as a leader or boss, your every move is on the spotlight. People will pay attention to how you speak to your juniors, how you show care and consideration for others, how you manage stressful situations, and even how you manage yourself. Your teams will also look to you to model the kind of behavior that they should emulate and to be their mentor in matters of business and relationships. Imagine being in such a position while lacking emotional intelligence. More likely than not, you are going to be highly overwhelmed.

That being said, everyone needs emotional intelligence in their lives. You do not need to be anybody's boss to appreciate the benefits that come with being self-aware and self-regulating. And what about motivation? Everyone could use some bit of intrinsic drive and passion in their lives. Motivation is what gives you the fuel to get you everything that you need in your life. If not for anything else, aim to be emotionally intelligent so that you can have better personal relationships in your life. We could all use some of those.

CHAPTER 14 - THINGS THAT YOU NEED TO STOP DOING NOW

In developing your emotional intelligence, there are things that you should start and stop doing, things that are not obvious but have a big impact, like little drops of water compared to an ocean. As small as they are, each of them incrementally makes a big impact on your growth, both positively and negatively, and if it's the latter, it might be too late to fix the issue. It's not enough to know just how you can grow your emotional intelligence. It's important to note the things you do that tampers with the growth and begin stopping them, not tomorrow or next week—now!

How Do You Know These Things?

Some of the things that tamper with the growth of your emotional intelligence hide in between everyday habits that are considered normal by you, so finding them out can be a tad bit difficult for you. When there are certain things about you that put people off constantly, it's important to note that these things are detrimental to the growth of your emotional intelligence.

In finding these things out, pay attention to how you are viewed by people. It's okay to say, "I don't care about what others think of me or my lifestyle," but if the things you do that seemingly does not make a difference to you and negatively affects those around you, it's okay to start thinking about changing those things.

See how your actions reflect on others around you. In watching how these actions reflect on them, you are exposed to what you are doing that is detrimental to your own emotional intelligence, this is important because one of the characteristics of people with high emotional intelligence is the positive impact their actions have on those around them. So if your actions are constantly affecting those around you in a negative manner, that's one way to know which things should be stopped that affects the growth of your emotional intelligence.

You can also go as far as asking. Meet friends, people who are close to you, converse with them, and ask them, "How do my actions affect you?" "The things I do, do they hurt you?" "Am I insensitive?" Another characteristic of a person with high emotional intelligence is empathy. So when you are told that you do not know how to empathize, because of a certain thing you are doing, then know that that action is detrimental to the growth of your emotional intelligence.

Now to the things that you do that are detrimental to the growth of your emotional intelligence, the things that you need to stop doing now.

Subtle Bragging

Subtle bragging, or humblebragging, is the act of bragging in a way that is not exactly noticed as bragging. You don't realize you are bragging when you practice humblebragging, because by your standards you are just being modest. This is something we do among friends, sometimes innocently.

An example of subtle bragging is watching your friend talk about how bloated he feels and how his fitness regimen seems to not be working. At this point, the only thing you are supposed to offer is a word of advice on how he could start making his regimen work. Instead you start yapping on and on about your water therapy and how you eat right, your low carbs diet, how much time you spend at the gym, and then you go on to slap your abs and move your arms to expose your awesome biceps and end with this statement: "Even after all I've done, I still don't look as good as I want to." Although, you thought you looked and sounded modest but you weren't.

To shed more light on what subtle bragging is, let's take a look at another scenario. Your friend confided in you about a breakout on her skin because of the kind of product she is using. Instead of showing her empathy, or assisting her in getting help, you immediately refer to how you use organic products only, and that it's not even enough to give you what you want, then you say something like "I don't think I'm beautiful anyway," and then laugh sarcastically.

Anyone who heard the statements uttered in both scenarios may think you just wanted to list out your flaws, but sincerely, you just wanted to let your friend know that you had better skin or a better body. You just subtly bragged about your skin and your body structure and in the process subtly judged your friend for using chemical-based products to enhance skin beauty or not following his fitness regimen. You don't realize that this action you just carried out is bragging but in subtlety.

Those words were not needed. All you needed to do was offer a word of advice, but you slipped out on that and went straight to bragging subtly. It didn't seem like bragging because, well, you are friends; he knows you eat right, and it wouldn't hurt mentioning it one more time. But it did hurt. And most times, the people who get hurt do not say anything about it because how would they explain to the next person that they got hurt simply because you said "You ate right, and still didn't look good"? Most times, subtle bragging means you're looking for validation and it reduces the self-esteem of the recipient.

Being Overly Serious

This might look like a good trait because it yields productive results but it can be a problem in disguise. There's a difference between being serious and taking yourself too seriously, the latter is indicative of underlying insecurities that individuals may have, for instance humor may uncloak weaknesses which may leave them emotionally naked. Although it takes times to accept your own weaknesses, being too serious will leave no place for creating relationships. If you examine the relationships you have in your life and realize that you only have business inclined relationships then you might be exhibiting this trait.

Being too serious detaches you from your coworkers and friends. Nobody wants to say something funny they found online to you, because they would come off as not serious. You unknowingly miss out on the beautiful things of life and it might begin to reflect on your family and kids too. They cannot say, "Daddy, I saw and played with a clown today," because they know the only thing you want to see or talk about is their schoolwork.

You don't find yourself laughing at anything, because they seem mundane and too casual. So a joke is usually met with a harsh remark from you rather than a smile or laughter. Being overly serious is a bad thing, wrapped up in good results because it makes you unapproachable. It is bad for relationship building and should be stopped as soon as possible.

Going through Your Phone in the Middle of a Conversation

This is a very disrespectful act that is unfortunately very common nowadays. Some people are very attached to their phone that they can't bear to take their eyes off it for an hour, hence they tend to go through their phone even when an important meeting is going on. This can mess up your relationship because it makes the person think you're insensitive. Bringing out your phone and going through it in the middle of a conversation is not only insensitive but it's disrespectful too. At this point you're telling the person that whatever they were saying to you, as important as it was to them, is unimportant to you and that can make the person feel insignificant. You should definitely stop using your phone in the middle of a conversation.

Calling the Names of the Important People You Know

If you cannot go through a conversation without mentioning the names of the important people you know, this is you trying to make yourself look better than every other person sitting in that room at that moment and you do not necessarily have to drag that kind of attention to yourself. You have met the president—nice. Your father's brother is the one on TV—yeah, that's nice. Not everyone needs to know. Instead of making you look interesting, you come off as a braggart in want of attention, and that sincerely puts people off. Name dropping might make you feel better about yourself, but how do you think it will make others feel about you?

Screaming at People

No one likes a screamer. No matter how much the person deserves your screaming, it's not necessary. You make people feel small and insignificant when you scream at them. Especially when it is a constant habit of yours to scream when you are mad at others. You can say, it's just your way of reacting when you're mad, and all the screaming make you feel a lot better, but have you ever stopped to consider how the other person feels about your screaming?

Using Abusive Words When Angry

You cannot take words back, so when you are about to use abusive words in a fit of anger, rest assured they will go a long way to harm the person you are saying them to. You can say you don't mean them a lot later, but the words have already had their effects. Sometimes the use of hurtful words stems from a desire to make them feel the hurt you're feeling, but it's not really necessary.

Gossiping

"It was just a harmless conversation," you would say. But it did involve you talking to one person about another and spilling secrets that you were meant to keep. It did involve you saying things that were not exactly great about another person. Now, exactly how harmless was that conversation again?

When you gossip about another person, it says more about you than it does about the person you were talking about. It doesn't make sense to base your discussion on the life of another, relationships that thrive on gossip have a very shaky foundation and are bound to crash sooner than later. Gossiping is a horrible habit, and it depicts a very low state of emotional intelligence.

There are a ton of other things you could talk about when chilling with friends. It doesn't necessarily have to be about that other people. Unless you are talking about ways to help them, there is no need talking about their situation. People make an interesting topic, but it's not a topic that really needs to be discussed. It's an addictive habit, and soon you'd be talking about the person talking to you to another when you run out of people to talk about. Gossips depicts disloyalty so it should be avoided at all cost.

Talking a Lot More Than Listening

When you talk more than you listen, it limits your chances at learning and unlearning things. You are literally shoving your opinion down the throat of others without giving them the time or the chance to air theirs. This is an attitude that repels people. For communication to occur, there has to be more than talking, and there has to be listening too. And when you talk more than you listen, communication has not taken place, because you were the only one talking.

Listening most times helps you to make a better decision. Not listening to people when they talk and being too concerned about airing your own opinion will make you look ignorant. At some point, you will begin to say things that do not make a lot of sense because you were not listening in the first place. You will suddenly begin to look ignorant, and no one wants to associate with an ignorant person who is also not willing to learn.

Posting Too Much of Yourself on Social Media

A lot of people are guilty of this action. It depicts a want for acceptance, and it's usually captured by the phrase "putting it all out there." Well, news flash, you do not have to do this. You do not necessarily have to tell the world all the dreams you have or all the things you do before you wake up and before you go to bed. You do not need to be validated by social media and those online. They don't care about you. They should not know so much about you. It's needless throwing these things in their faces. Save some information for yourself. Remember, the Internet has a good memory; it never forgets.

Saying Too Much of Yourself Too Early in a Relationship

Not everyone needs to know all the information you spill to them when you are talking to them for the first time. Sharing too much too early makes you come off as an attention seeker. It seems like you want the person to think you are real and open and want them to like you almost immediately. It's a lot better to let the relationship flow organically, and these other bits of yourself that you're so eager to give up will come out naturally without stress. It's also better to relax and try to know the other person better too while trying to build trust in the relationship. Sharing too much of yourself is rushing things and is not giving the other person a chance to be comfortable enough in the relationship.

Being Closed-minded

This is a very big problem. It is important that you view things with an open mind. Keeping a closed mind makes you unapproachable. It also means that you already have a formed opinion about a certain thing, and when you are approached, you are unwilling to listen and make changes to your initial thoughts, making you inaccessible by anyone. It's very sensible to keep an open mind and be open to changes. Learn to see the world from the eyes of other people. It makes you more sensitive.

These habits are associated with people with low emotional intelligence, and they should be stopped now. They are harmful to you, to the people around you, and to the growth of your emotional intelligence.

CHAPTER 15 - PRACTICE FOR PERFECTION

You have been exposed to the meaning and importance of emotional intelligence all through this book. The skills you need to acquire and the things you need to do to develop your EQ have also been discussed extensively.

Below are some exercises that can help you master your emotions:

Always Have a Plan B

The reason you feel dejected and frustrated such that you take it out on others is probably because you know you don't have any other option apart from the current one. Hence, if the plan fails, you feel like your world is crashing down around you. You cannot afford to put all your eggs in one basket in life because life is way too risky for that kind of action. When you have a plan, you will always be afraid of the outcome of your decisions but having an alternative plan gives you peace of mind.

A plan B is not even good enough; you should have a plan B, C, D, E, F..., and Z. So, as you invest in that business, also look out for another business you can also invest your money in. In case you don't get the kind of yield you expect from that business, you will have another option you can look forward to. Some people see having other options as being afraid but that is not true. Having other alternatives is being shrewd. There will never be any time you will be at the mercy of anyone when you can access other options.

Stress Management Skills

Stress can make you anxious or nervous. It is okay to be anxious or nervous once in a while because of the sensitivity of a task you need to carry out. However, it becomes an issue when you are unable to perform as you ought because you are nervous. You can reduce anxiety by reducing your temperature. You can drink some cold water to help with this. You can also reduce the rate at which you consume caffeine to help with this.

Caffeine is a stimulant and can increase your anxiety level when not properly handled. Hence, you can stay off caffeine or reduce the quantity of your intake during periods when you need to handle situations that are tense. Simple things such as these will improve the way you handle yourself and others. The most important things in life are not necessarily complicated things but simple things you feel are too simple to be taken seriously.

Try Aerobic Exercises

Aerobic exercises can help you reduce fear and depression. You will be surprised to find out that you will be able to dissipate negative emotions as you move your body. Your calmness will return and you will be able to think clearly again. These exercises affect your heart rate and also make your circulatory system continue to function the way it ought to function. Examples of such exercises include taking a brisk walk or skipping with a jump rope.

Reduce the Use of Sentences That Begin With "You"

This comes in and when you feel that you are not getting what you deserve from a person or from a corporate body. Sentences that start with "you" during those moments often lead to pointing an accusing finger which makes people uncomfortable. You will be reducing your chances of getting what you want when you talk that way, especially to people who are superior and have the capacity to deny you or delay your entitlements.

By simply addressing the situation without pointing accusing fingers shows to them that you understand the situation in spite of the fact that you have not gotten what you want. Avoiding sentences that start with "you" will help you to avoid becoming defensive which pisses off people. When you are defensive, you will only see the faults of others and neglect yours. Instead of saying "you have not been listening to me", you can say "I would appreciate if you can hear me out please".

Those listening to you will also not be defensive when you don't point accusing fingers at them. They will want to hear you out and will most likely be ready to negotiate with you and even make compromises when they see that you are not making them responsible for the unpleasant situation you have found yourself in. This will not take anything from you, it will only allow you to reduce the rate of having to deal with negative emotions accusations often generate.

Take a Deep Breath During Tense Situations

There is no way you can escape having one or two difficult people in your endeavors in life. If you are lucky not to have such people as your spouse, they could be your boss or work under you. You will definitely come across such people at one point or the other. Hence, it is better to determine long beforehand what you will do when you come across such people rather than hope you will never have an encounter with them.

During tense moments when you feel like speaking in annoyance, learn to take deep breaths and slowly count to ten. You will have a better grip on your emotions when you do this. You will think about other means of resolving the situation during this moment and find an alternative dispute resolution rather than speak out of anger. Words spoken out of anger are usually "poisonous" and intended to hurt the other person.

Most times, even when you are in the right, you will end up regretting the things you say because you are angry. When you are angry, you are likely going to reveal secrets the person kept with you before your annoyance. You will go all out to hurt the person and this will not help you or the people around you.

Don't Hold Back Compliments

You will often be told not to let out negative emotions but it is equally important to let out positive emotions. I mean, always look out for opportunities to tell people good things about them. Tell people they have done well when they are doing well and mean it. When you tell people that they are doing well when they are not doing well, you are not helping them. It is mere flattery and they will eventually mark you out as an insincere person in the long run.

Hence, you don't have to go overboard. Simply look out for the right things they do and sincerely compliment them about those things. Let people around you know they are looking good. It helps boost their confidence and perceive you as a positive person. When you have a culture of telling people they are doing well when they do will make them open to hear you when you point out the areas that they need to improve. They will not see you as someone who is criticizing them to make them feel bad.

Listen and Truly Listen

It is one thing to listen hypocritically to people so that they will not accuse you of not listening to them, it is another thing to listen to people because you want to hear them objectively. There are different reasons that people listen. Some people listen so as to be able to find loopholes to attack the person they are listening to. You should not do this because it is not helpful. You will totally miss out on anything the person has to say that can help you get better.

You should listen to people because you are interested in whatever they have to say. Practicing active listening shows you are humble and don't see other people as nonentities. When people around you notice that you listen to them to combat them, they will be reluctant to tell you things even when they feel it will help you. They will also be reluctant to open up to you about themselves.

Conclusion

I hope you enjoyed reading it and were learned the finer nuances of emotional intelligence, self-awareness, regulation of emotions and social relationships. I also hope it gave you plenty of actionable ideas, practical pointers and wisdom nuggets about increasing your emotional quotient or emotional intelligence.

The best part is that unlike intelligence quotient, emotional quotient can be developed over a period of time through regular practice, effort, training, and implementation. Enhancing our emotional intelligence is a constantly evolving and dynamic process that helps us grow our psychological and social abilities with time.

Emotions are never easy to understand. That is because for most of our lives, we have let them manage us. We haven't taken the time to understand them because we are too distracted by events that are happening around us.

We are busy at work. We have bills to pay. We are worried about our family.

But the important thing to realize is that if we do not set aside the time to manage our emotions, then we are always going to be stuck in an endless loop of negative emotions. We will never get the opportunity to break free and truly work towards things that add purpose to our lives and make us happier.

And before we know it, we have already wasted most of our lives playing catch-up to our emotions. Our emotions are powerful, and they are also necessary. Without them, we might not be able to navigate the complexities of life. But the key takeaway here is that we have to use emotions to help us go through life. We should be able to understand how they influence our lives.

You are not meant to merely survive life. You are meant to live it. And the first step towards living your life is to manage one of its most vital components:

Your emotions.

The next step is to go out there and apply all the proven tips mentioned in this book. You cannot expect to become more emotionally intelligent by reading about it. Implement the techniques mentioned in the book in your daily life to notice the difference.

You'll slowly transform from an emotionally average or incompetent person who probably struggles with his/her and other's emotions to an emotionally developed and socially adept person, who will enjoy more fulfilling interpersonal relationships and professional success.

…………..

www.ingramcontent.com/pod-product-compliance
Lightning Source LLC
LaVergne TN
LVHW022048200926
848481LV00003B/821